T0301745

WEALTH
WISDOM
FOR EVERYONE

An Easy-to-Use Guide to Personal Financial
Planning and Wealth Creation

Raffles Family Wealth and Legacy Series

Series Editor: Mark Haynes Daniell
(*Chairman, Raffles Family Wealth Trust Pte Ltd, Singapore*)

Published

Vol. 2 *Wealth Wisdom for Everyone: An Easy-to-Use Guide to Personal Financial Planning and Wealth Creation — Special Edition for the Raffles Wealth and Legacy Series*
by Mark Haynes Daniell & Karin Sixl-Daniell

Vol. 1 *Strategy for the Wealthy Family: Seven Principles to Assure Riches to Riches Across Generations*
by Mark Haynes Daniell

Other Book by Mark Haynes Daniell Published by World Scientific

---

World of Risk: A New Approach to Global Strategy and Leadership
ISBN: 978-981-238-758-5
ISBN: 978-981-238-759-2 (pbk)

WEALTH WISDOM
FOR EVERYONE

An Easy-to-Use Guide to Personal Financial
Planning and Wealth Creation

Mark Haynes Daniell
The Raffles Family Wealth Trust Pte Ltd, Singapore

Karin Sixl-Daniell

World Scientific

W JERSEY · LONDON · SINGAPORE · BEIJING · SHANGHAI · HONG KONG · TAIPEI · CHENNAI · TOKYO

Published by

World Scientific Publishing Co. Pte. Ltd.

5 Toh Tuck Link, Singapore 596224

USA office: 27 Warren Street, Suite 401-402, Hackensack, NJ 07601

UK office: 57 Shelton Street, Covent Garden, London WC2H 9HE

British Library Cataloguing-in-Publication Data
A catalogue record for this book is available from the British Library.

Raffles Family Wealth and Legacy Series — Vol. 2
WEALTH WISDOM FOR EVERYONE
An Easy-to-Use Guide to Personal Financial Planning and Wealth Creation —
Special Edition for the Raffles Wealth and Legacy Series

ISBN 978-981-125-901-2 (hardcover)
ISBN 978-981-125-924-1 (paperback)
ISBN 978-981-125-902-9 (ebook for institutions)
ISBN 978-981-125-903-6 (ebook for individuals)

For any available supplementary material, please visit
https://www.worldscientific.com/worldscibooks/10.1142/12909#t=suppl

Desk Editors: Venkatesh Sandhya/Nicole Ong

Typeset by Stallion Press
Email: enquiries@stallionpress.com

Printed in Singapore

ABOUT THE AUTHORS

Mark Haynes Daniell is the Founder and Chairman of the Raffles Family Wealth Trust Pte Ltd, based in Singapore, a boutique advisory firm focused on Ultra-High Net Worth families and their businesses. He is also the founder of the newly launched e-learning site www.raffleslegacylearning. com, which provides a comprehensive suite of learning opportunities for ultra-high net worth families, their employees and their advisors. He is joined in this initiative by a team of acknowledged global experts in the areas essential to help legacy families to preserve their wealth and strengthen their families, with a particular focus on family leaders and members of the rising generation.

Topics addressed in the courses and individual lessons on that site include: Family History, Purpose, Vision and Values; Family Governance, Leadership and Succession; Family Business Ownership and Strategy, Family Wealth Management; Family Wealth Structuring and Value

Preservation; Philanthropy and Social Engagement; Family Dynamics: Culture, Relationships, Disputes and Individual Issues; NextGen Education, Generational Transitions and other topics relevant to the creation, preservation and transition of family wealth.

The Raffles Family Wealth and Legacy Series of books accompany and enrich the online learning experience available in that site, and include the following titles available from the World Scientific Publishing Corporation:

Wealth Wisdom for Everyone
Strategy for the Wealthy Family
Family Legacy and Leadership
Family Wealth Management
Family Wealth and Legacy Planning
Family Business Strategy World of Risk

Mr Daniell has also authored two books on business strategy published by Palgrave Macmillan entitled *Strategy: A Step-by-Step Approach to the Development and Presentation of World Class Business Strategy* and *The Elements of Strategy: A Pocket Guide to the Essence of Successful Business Strategy.*

Mr Daniell's books have won many awards and received many positive reviews, including from the Harvard Business School, and his first book was selected as a Sunday Times (London) Business Book of the Week.

In addition to his current positions, Mr Daniell is a former senior partner at Bain & Company, Director of investment bank Wasserstein Perella in London and Paris and President of KI ventures, a strategic investment company listed on the main board of the Singapore Stock Exchange. Mr Daniell has been a frequent guest on the BBC, CNBC, CNN, Channel NewsAsia and Bloomberg TV channels. He has spoken at the World Economic Forum, The Royal

Institute for International Affairs and many other global conferences.

Mr Daniell is a graduate of the Harvard Law School (Juris Doctor), Oxford University (University College, BA/MA, Marshall Scholar), Amherst College (BA magna cum laude, Phi Beta Kappa, Deans List, other prizes and scholarships), and the Phillips Exeter Academy (High Honours and National Merit Scholar). He has also attended the Université de Paris IV–Sorbonne (D.E.F. 1er and 2e degrees) and the Institut d'Etudes Politiques de Paris (C.E.P.).

Dr mag. Mas. Karin Sixl-Daniell has a depth of experience as a university business school professor and lecturer in Austria, and in numerous online international educational initiatives. In addition to her undergraduate and graduate degrees from the University of Graz, she holds a Master's degree in health care management from the Danube University Krems, also in Austria.

CONTENTS

STATEMENT OF PURPOSE

Wealth Wisdom for Everyone provides a series of insights, observations and useful forms to help you to manage your own financial affairs and pursue your own financial objectives.

The contents of this book, the Primetime Morning TV show and all associated communications are intended for general educational purposes only. *Wealth Wisdom for Everyone,* in all of its forms, should not be construed as investment, financial or legal advice.

Any decision to invest (or not to invest) in a specific opportunity is an individual decision, which should be taken only after consultation with a qualified professional accountant, banker, broker or financial planner.

ACKNOWLEDGEMENTS

The authors would like to express their appreciation to all those who made *Wealth Wisdom for Everyone* possible.

Our guest financial experts on each of Channel NewsAsia's Primetime Morning *Wealth Wisdom for Everyone* TV segments were all insightful, patient and interesting. Each and every guest made a substantial contribution to the overall series of television segments and to this book. We would like to thank:

Segment	Guest Expert
Budgeting and Trusts & Estate Planning	Juliana Ng, Director of Tax – International Private Wealth Services, Ernst & Young
Income Expectations & Career Management	Davy Lau, Managing Partner, Egon Zehnder International

Taxes	Wu Soo Mee, Director of Human Capital, Ernst & Young
Expenses	Sarah Mavrinac, Assistant Professor, INSEAD
Insurance	Roger Yeh, Founder and Owner, Raksa Pratikara Insurance
Mortgages and Credit Cards & Consumer Finance	Arthur Douglas Lim, CEO, Alpha Financial Advisers
Educational Finance	Nicholas Hadow, Regional Sales Director, Aberdeen Asset Management
Charity & Philanthropy	Mrs Tan Chee Koon, CEO, National Volunteer & Philanthropy Centre
Savings & Investments	Nicholas Tan, Head of Group Wealth Management, OCBC Bank Singapore
Asset Allocation	Robin Tomlin, Vice Chairman-Asia, UBS Investment Bank
Business Assets	Philip Anderson, INSEAD Alumni Fund Chaired Professor of Entrepreneurship
Local & International Shares and Derivatives, Options & Hedges	AST Rajan, Managing Director, Aquarius Investment Advisors
Bonds, Fixed Income & REITs	Simon Goh, Vice President, Head of Investment and Specialized Products, ABN AMRO

Mutual Funds & Unit Trusts	Tom Tobin, Head of Personal Financial Services, HSBC
Pensions	Peter Tan, Group Financial Services Director, Prudential
Foreign Currencies	Thio Chin Loo, Senior Currency Strategist, BNP Paribas
Gold & Commodities	Sunny Verghese, Group Managing Director and CEO, Olam International
Art, Antiques & Wine	Pierre Baer, Executive Director & Regional Head of Marketing, SG Private Banking (Asia Pacific)
Contingency Planning	Anil Gaba, The Orpar Chaired Professor of Risk Management INSEAD

We would also like to thank the people who worked so hard on the other side of the cameras from Channel NewsAsia's *Primetime Morning* — Susanna Kulatissa, Senior Executive Producer and cameramen Aminuddin Bin Abu and Mohd Radzu — to bring *Wealth Wisdom for Everyone* to so many viewers.

Suzanne Jung anchored each and every segment with elegance and intelligence, no easy task with so many guests across so many diverse topics.

Ines Craig provided much appreciated support at some of the busiest times. Her effort to help us all throughout the process was very much appreciated.

We would particularly like to thank Hilary Galea, tireless editor from The Cuscaden Group, without whose dedication and high standards the show and this book would not have been possible.

And finally, the authors would like to thank the extraordinary team at World Scientific Publishing, led by Chean Chian Cheong, who was able to bring this book from concept to market in an amazingly short time. It was a pleasure to have worked with them all.

CHANNEL NEWSASIA AND PRIMETIME MORNING

This book, *Wealth Wisdom for Everyone*, was produced in conjunction with a featured weekly segment by the same name for Primetime Morning, the leading morning show on Channel NewsAsia aired daily from 6:30 a.m. to 9:30 a.m., Singapore/ Hong Kong time.

Channel NewsAsia is a pan-Asian news channel based in Singapore and owned by Mediacorp. Started on March 1st 1999, the channel is now seen in more than 20 Asian territories. It is beamed on the AsiaSat 3 satellite and available free to air in Singapore as well as on MediaCorp's TVMobile service on SBS Transit public buses and selected locales.

Primetime Morning offers news, analysis and live interview segments every day, serving the information needs of its viewers for headline news, in-depth financial commentary and lifestyle coverage. On Primetime Morning you are updated with the latest developments around the world from the people who know best — so that you're already ahead of the crowd when you head out the door in the morning.

Wealth Wisdom for Everyone is a multi-media project. Apart from this book, the weekly segments are screened over a six month period on Channel NewsAsia's Primetime Morning and the information is found on channelnewsasia.com. There are also related conferences and other initiatives to bring you the maximum benefit for your own financial planning efforts.

Please check local listings to see when *Wealth Wisdom for Everyone* will be broadcast in your own area.

∞ 1 ∞

INTRODUCTION

The creation of material wealth and an increase in financial prosperity are goals to which most people aspire, no matter what their current situation.

The rich want to become richer. The poor want to become financially secure. Those in between want to move higher up the ladder of financial success.

Financial security also provides a way for us to fulfil broader family or community responsibilities and to realise our broader aspirations, creating a better future for those who depend on us. Greater wealth can create greater security for our parents and greater opportunities for our children.

Although almost all of us aspire to be wealthier than we are, many of us are frustrated in our pursuit of this goal by a sense of unrealised potential, of lost opportunity and lack of control over our own financial destinies.

What few of us realise is that, with a little understanding and basic planning, we already hold the key to achieving greater wealth without having to work even harder or earn even more. What is important is learning how to make our money work better for us.

Wealth Wisdom for Everyone provides us with a set of practical tools to create, manage, protect and grow our own personal wealth in a more efficient manner: The Annual Budget, Monthly Budget Tracker, Personal Wealth Schedule and Total Family Wealth forms attached at the back of this book can be completed to help you develop your own unique Wealth Wisdom Plan.

Throughout this book you will also be presented with insights and ideas which can provide answers to such questions as:

- *Where can I best invest my money so it achieves the objectives I set for myself?*
- *What are the biggest mistakes people usually make in investing? Why is that? How can I avoid these mistakes?*
- *How should we think about managing our careers — is maximising next year's income the best way to build wealth? If not, what is the best approach to career management?*
- *When should I start saving?*
- *Are there any practical ideas I can use to start to teach my children or grandchildren about financial responsibility? About social responsibility?*
- *What is the right level of expense?*
- *How much money should I save to achieve my financial objectives?*
- *Who should do a financial plan?*
- *When do I need to redo my financial plan?*

- *Is having a will enough, or should I do more for estate planning?*

By reading and applying the contents of *Wealth Wisdom for Everyone*, you will be well placed to answer these questions from an informed position and you will have in hand many of the tools and approaches needed to improve the content and value of your own unique financial plan.

As the experts remind us, if you don't control your finances, they will control you.

Part I

WEALTH WISDOM FOR YOU

◌❨ 2 ❩◌

YOUR WEALTH CHECK

Many of us make New Year's resolutions to lose weight, give up smoking or learn a new language, which we hope will lead to a healthier and more rewarding lifestyle. Perhaps fewer of us make resolutions which will lead to an improvement in our finances and a better attitude towards the sound management of our money, which can also lead to the same result.

Just as it is important to have regular health check-ups, even when we feel fine, we should have a wealth check-up at least once a year. We should also review and adjust our plans if there is a major upheaval or change in our personal circumstances, such as a marriage, house purchase, birth of a child, change of job, divorce or retirement.

TIME FOR A CHECK-UP?

To decide whether it is time for a wealth check and a new wealth plan, the following questions can serve as a guide:

- Do you have an understanding of your financial needs — now and in the future?
- Do you have a clear set of financial objectives?
- Do you have a written financial plan?
- Do you have savings and investment targets?
- Did you meet those targets last year?
- Have you documented all of your expenses and reviewed them for potential savings?
- Are all your expenses fully understood and under control?
- Will your current savings and investment rate make it possible for you to achieve your investment targets?
- Are you content with your current salary and future salary prospects?
- Do you have a contingency plan for emergencies?
- Do you have adequate life insurance?
- Do you have a will?
- Do you have a retirement plan?
- Do you have a clear understanding of your retirement needs?
- Do you have a clear understanding of your retirement income?
- Will your pension adequately cover your retirement needs?
- Are you satisfied that your finances are fully under control and that your money is working for you?

ELEMENTS OF A WEALTH CHECK

If you have answered 'no' to any of these questions, or if you are facing a significant change in your life stage or financial circumstances, it may be time to review and amend your plans to take into account the new situation.

Before updating your existing plan, or designing your first Wealth Wisdom Plan, it is important to complete a wealth check to identify your needs and investment objectives.

Wealth checks, whether conducted on-line or face-to-face, will lead to a unique model based upon your own situation and set to achieve your own objectives.

It is advisable not only to conduct a wealth check every year, but also to ensure that this particular resolution does not suffer the same unhappy neglect as so many other forgotten New Year's resolutions.

AVOID THE 'FIRE, READY, AIM' SYNDROME

It is always important to think before we act. The 'fire, ready, aim' approach is not often the best way to hit your financial targets.

An informed and systematic approach to financial management is a more certain way to accomplish your goals. The best proven approach, taken by the world's wealthiest investors (and their advisers), is to pursue the goal of wealth maximization through a disciplined approach to financial management and decision-making. The result of better decisions and better management is a fully implemented wealth creation plan which is both efficient and effective.

Efficient means that no money is wasted, that after-tax income is maximised and unnecessary expenses are avoided. Efficient also means that the return on savings and investment is optimized and that your money is placed where it can earn the most appropriate return, given your personal objectives.

Effective means that the plan achieves the goals it sets out to achieve. The importance of specific goals will vary by individual and by life stage. A single young person living at home or a retired couple will have very different priorities from a married couple with two children. An effective plan will ensure that you are able to achieve your most important objectives; these could include purchasing a first home, providing an education for your children and grandchildren or ensuring that you and your spouse can look forward to a worry-free retirement.

If you are not yet satisfied that you are fully fit on the financial front, then it may well be time to address the shortfalls in your own approach.

It is only through thoughtful preparation, coupled with effective action, that we can achieve the kind of fitness we seek.

❦ 3 ❦

YOUR WEALTH OBJECTIVES

Almost everything begins with self-knowledge and awareness.

Building wealth and planning for a sound financial future is no exception. Our personal beliefs, experiences and influences will all be important in shaping our investment style, wealth goals and specific wealth objectives.

Two components of our Wealth Wisdom Plans which will address, in financial terms, who we are, how we want to move forward and where we want to go are:

- Our personal investment profile, and
- Our specific wealth objectives.

DETERMINING YOUR PERSONAL INVESTMENT PROFILE

Your personal investment profile, or personal investment style, will determine the general approach you adopt to set priorities and select investments. A personal investment profile will capture three traditional key variables: the *time frame* over which you want to invest, your *attitude to risk* and your *liquidity preference.*

To make your personal investment profile more useful in determining your ultimate wealth objectives, we have added two other dimensions to the three mentioned above: *rate of savings* and the *need for contingency.* Each of these dimensions is explained more fully below:

Time frame: In every case, deciding on the time frame for your plan is important. The time frame for your financial plan will determine when your financial vision should begin and end.

You may want to set out a detailed plan from now to age 70. Alternatively, you may want only to have a three-year plan to ensure you have sufficient funds to make a down-payment on a new car or home. A family may want a plan from today until the end of the children's education. The content of a plan will vary substantially by the time frame you choose for the overall plan or for individual components within it.

Risk appetite: There is no such thing as a low-risk/high-return investment. If you are told an investment opportunity is 'too good to be true', it probably is. The financial markets work far too efficiently to allow high, risk-free returns to investors.

As part of the process of assessing your own investment profile and setting your own financial objectives, you will need to specify the level of risk you are willing to take. This risk appetite will, in all likelihood, vary over time.

The couple facing retirement may want to avoid as much risk as possible to ensure they are comfortable in their golden years. The young and carefree single person just starting out may be willing to spend a higher proportion of income on education or entertainment, or take more investment risk.

As well as opening ourselves up to investment-related risk, we must also avoid the real financial risk we take by being complacent, making false economies or just trusting in luck. For example, we are taking financial risk by building in a low savings rate, skimping on insurance, counting on a weak pension system to take care of us in old age, or depending upon family financial reserves which could be eaten up by protracted healthcare costs or lost through imprudent investment.

Liquidity preference: The value you place on having cash in hand, the degree of ease with which you want to be able to access your money, or your preference for income over gain, is called a 'liquidity preference'. Having a preference for money to be available on demand (i.e. a high liquidity preference) will mean a more limited set of savings and investment alternatives — and a lower return on your investment — than if you are willing to tie up your money in longer-term investments (i.e. you have a low liquidity preference).

Savings rate: Our savings rate is the percentage of income we put aside for investment or savings after covering all expenses. The actual rate can be high (a conservative saver preparing for the future) or very low (someone setting nothing aside for the future). Our appetite for saving and investment is, in our view, as important as our appetite for risk in determining our financial health and defining our wealth prospects.

Contingency needs: Our financial plans will need to allow for a degree of redirection and unexpected change. We cannot know everything in advance; we will encounter unexpected events, good and bad, along the way. That's just the way life is.

As a result, we will need to leave some financial room to accommodate that unexpected change. How much we need to set aside will depend upon the likelihood of some negative event occurring in the future. A conservative saver will set aside three to six months' salary for contingency. Others, less concerned about something disrupting their financial lives, will set aside nothing for contingency.

In some ways, these last two categories are both reflections of our views on risk, but their importance amongst other variables for a Wealth Wisdom Plan led us to single them out for your consideration.

Your investment profile forms part of the Personal Wealth Schedule found at the back of this book. Complete each line on that form by circling the answer which best describes your attitude or approach to each of the five criteria listed in the left hand column of the table below.

The pattern determined by your answers will give you an idea of the kind of investor you are likely to be.

Personal Investment Profile (circle one for each category)			
Time Frame	short	medium	long
Risk Appetite	low	medium	high
Liquidity Preference	high	medium	low
Savings Rate	low	medium	high
Contingency Needs	high	medium	low

Translating your profile

Note that the order of answers is not always the same. In essence, however, the further to the right your circled answers fall, the higher your wealth creation potential is likely to be.

There is no right or wrong profile. There will almost certainly be times when it is more appropriate for your answers to fall further towards the left-hand side of the matrix than the right.

Going back to our earlier examples, the couple facing retirement are likely to have significantly more circles on the left of the matrix than the young carefree person with a higher risk appetite and a longer time frame in which to revise and adjust his or her Personal Wealth Plan.

Based on the personal investment profile we choose, there are very different approaches to investing, with very different implications.

Investment approach

As you work through the chapters of *Wealth Wisdom for Everyone*, you will be able to develop a clear sense of how your own personal investment profile will operate in practice and can apply your own unique approach to investment decisions. Your investment profile is likely to reflect a combination of the basic investment approaches described below:

Income generation: An income generation approach may focus more on savings and deposit products, investments with a high income yield such as a REIT (see Chapter 19: Property), a high-dividend-yielding share portfolio or a tenanted property producing regular payments.

This approach could be appropriate for an older couple nearing retirement or a more conservative younger investor.

Capital growth: At the other end of the spectrum, and perhaps more appropriate for a younger person or a working couple with income well in excess of expenses, a capital growth approach places a higher priority on increasing the value of investments instead of the income they can generate.

This approach may focus on a higher percentage of shares and products with greater risk attached, such as emerging markets products, commodities, new property developments and other investments where short-term income generation is not a key priority.

Balanced approach: For many people, the overall objective of a savings and investment portfolio is neither purely income nor solely capital growth. For most of us, finding a balance between the two may be the right path to follow. As a result of pursuing a balanced model of income and growth, investors can accumulate a blend of savings and investment products which creates both short-term income and long-term capital growth.

This balanced approach may be appropriate for people in the middle stages of their lives, or those who do not have a particularly strong preference for income or growth at a set point in time.

SETTING YOUR SPECIFIC WEALTH OBJECTIVES

Having defined the characteristics that best describe your personal investment profile and translated that insight into a description of your approach to investment, you are now ready to set out your specific wealth objectives.

Those goals can be top-down, as in "I would like to double my net worth in five years", to very specific "I would like to have saved $5,000 in two years", to very long term "I would like to retire on $25,000 per year and leave my house and $500,000 to my children after I am gone".

For every individual or family, there are likely to be specific objectives which can be accomplished through better financial management and through an allocation of part of a portfolio of assets to achieve a specific goal.

For example, a family may be saving to pay for a wedding in a year's time and will therefore require a certain amount of money in their home currency on a particular day. They may want to set up a dedicated savings account for that purpose.

Another family may be seeking to educate a child abroad, which will require a substantial payment in British Pounds or

US Dollars across many years in the future. They may want to set up a mutual fund in the currency of the country in which their child is most likely to attend university and a long-term savings account (e.g. in certificates of deposit) in the same currency.

These objectives are all very clear and concise, as objectives should be. What is also important in determining your wealth objectives is to select only a few, high priorities and to articulate them in a clear and unambiguous manner.

Business school wisdom tells us that our goals should be SMART: Specific, Measurable, Achievable, Realistic and Time- specified. This test is well worth applying to your own wealth objectives. Your personal investment profile will help you to ensure that your actual objectives are consistent with your selected investment strategy.

On Form III, your Personal Wealth Schedule, you should enter your own, high priority, SMART wealth objectives.

Wealth Objectives
1.
2.
3.

IMPLEMENTING YOUR OBJECTIVES

Having specified your wealth objectives, you will now be able to use them to guide your own individual plans and actions. Only through disciplined implementation of our strategies are we most likely to achieve the full set of objectives we set for ourselves.

Perhaps as important as knowing what to do, having a clear strategy will also tell us what *not* to do. If we are to pursue a focused, medium-risk, income-generating investment strategy, then we should turn away high-risk, illiquid investments or long-term capital gain initiatives.

Only by action consistent with our strategies and supportive of the achievement of our goals can we get where we want to go.

A Seamless Flow

In order to ensure that your personal investment profile, your wealth objectives and your savings and investment portfolio are fully coordinated, all three are included in your Personal Wealth Schedule, Form III.

Even though your specific objectives will change over time, your current plan should always support the achievement of your current objectives. You can change your plan when you change your objectives; you can save more (or less) at different stages of your life. You can make investments with greater risk (but also potentially greater return) more comfortably at some times than at others.

At each life stage, we will have different obligations and different opportunities. A Wealth Wisdom Plan will ensure that we fulfil our obligations and take advantage of the opportunities that are presented to us as best we can.

A well-thought-through plan, fully aligned to meet our objectives, can help us to aim carefully at, and have a far greater chance of hitting, the wealth targets we set for ourselves.

∽ 4 ∾

YOUR WEALTH WISDOM PLAN

Once your personal wealth objectives have been clarified, you are ready to set out the content of your own Wealth Wisdom Plan to pursue the objectives and achieve the targets you have set for yourself. The forms provided at the end of this book make up the heart of a clear and simple plan which will allow you to create, manage, protect and grow your own personal wealth.

It is always important to document your financial plans; only by having a clear and unambiguous plan covering all aspects of your financial life can you be sure that you are in control of all aspects of your finances. Leaving anything out can be a costly error as this may mean that investment accounts are not reviewed and managed properly, or small amounts of expense pass by unnoticed and build up over time. Hidden bank charges, unnecessary credit card interest payments and other items that could be better managed, or even eliminated altogether, should be captured in one complete system.

On Wisdom and Intelligence

Wisdom and intelligence are not the same thing. Your Wealth Wisdom Plan requires both.

Wisdom, in the context of a Wealth Wisdom Plan, is the knowledge gained over many years that can provide the principles, the values and the structure of your plan. Wisdom is achieved as much by reflection as it is by action.

Intelligence comes in two forms. On the one hand it is the specific knowledge we need to complete the forms that accompany this book. On the other hand it is the information required to decide on the best approach and to adjust those plans as appropriate going forward.

With your objectives clarified and your plans documented, you will have taken a major step forward to ensure that you control your finances — and not the other way around.

Getting Organised

Even before picking up our sharpened pencils or firing up the PC to fill out the forms accompanying this book, it is essential to organise our documents to make the job easier. With everything we need at hand, we can begin to put our financial affairs in order.

Assembling and organising the right set of documents has many benefits. Tax filings are easier. Mortgage applications can be made more quickly. Estate planning is clearer.

The Wealth Wisdom approach recommends that you divide your documents into two different groups. Broadly speaking, the first group of documents includes items which provide the data to help you make your plan. The second group will include the deeds, certificates, and ownership documents which will help to define your assets and liabilities. These original documents are of real value in their own right.

Both groups of documents can be personally sensitive. Their confidentiality should be protected by returning them to their rightful place at the end of each use.

Group one: planning documents

The first group includes regular account statements, expense information, photocopies of agreements and other relevant documents. These should be readily available at home or in your office — wherever you are most likely to do your personal financial planning.

These planning documents are primarily related to the Annual Budget form, and will also allow you to complete the Monthly Budget Tracker which reviews income and expenses on a regular basis.

These documents should be kept up to date by placing all new statements into a convenient folder as they arrive.

The items in this readily available file should include:

- Employment contracts (copies only)
- Pay slips with listed deductions
- Bank statements
- Brokerage account statements
- Credit card agreements
- Credit card statements
- Telecommunications agreements
- Telecommunications statements
- Utility bills
- Educational bills

- Domestic help forms and contracts
- Insurance documents (copies only)
- Club and association bills
- Pension fund statements
- Vehicle and transportation expense records
- Other key expense items files as needed
- Tax filings for past years
- Any other relevant documentation

And, for purposes of easy reference, you might also want to add to this file *photocopies* of:

- Birth certificates for all family members
- Marriage certificate (and divorce decrees if applicable)
- Military or national service documentation
- Educational diplomas, certificates and records
- Identity cards
- Religious records
- Credit and membership cards (with numbers to call in case of loss or theft)
- Share certificates
- Property deeds
- Mortgage documents
- Vehicle ownership documents
- Loan agreements
- Medical records
- Pet records
- Club and other association information
- List of key contacts (family, lawyer, accountant, doctor, etc)

Group two: important and original documents

The second group includes originals of important and valuable documents. The majority of these documents are related to the assets and liabilities categories listed in the Personal Wealth Schedule. Replacement of these items may be more difficult — or even costly — so their safety is essential. They should be kept in a secure, fireproof file, or perhaps even stored in a lawyer's office or somewhere away from your home to ensure their survival and easy access in your absence or during an emergency.

A passing note of caution may need to be added with regard to bank safe deposit boxes. Although both fireproof and tamper-proof in theory, placement of documents in a bank safe deposit box can create delays and difficulties in providing access for executors of estates and individuals other than the original renter of the safe deposit box.

Keys and box rental agreements can also go missing and require great care. If you do decide to place your valuables in a bank safe deposit box, make sure that you have a contingency plan that allows easy access should you no longer be able to access its contents for whatever reason.

Organising and keeping records safe is an important part of estate planning and wealth preservation — more than one large fortune has disappeared due to the inability of an owner or his heirs to access ownership documentation. Unclaimed assets in abandoned bank accounts and deposit boxes amount to billions of dollars around the world.

The estate of one very wealthy individual lost half its value when the owner died, having hidden important asset ownership papers out of fear they could be stolen and then forgetting to tell his heirs where they could find them. The heirs were never able to provide proof of ownership and therefore could not claim this very valuable part of their inheritance.

Let's make sure your own hard-earned wealth does not go missing in such a fashion.

Documents in this safe storage box should include *originals* of:

- Birth certificates for all family members
- Marriage certificate (and divorce decrees if applicable)
- Military or national service documentation
- Educational diplomas and certificates
- Religious records
- Share certificates
- Insurance policies (all kinds)
- Property deeds
- Mortgage documents
- Vehicle ownership documents
- Loan agreements
- Pension plan documentation
- Trust documents
- Will

Additionally, these important lists and documents should be included:

- A register of valuable personal items (e.g. art, furniture)
- List of other assets and liabilities
- Contracts and other documents relating to obligations
- List of key contacts (family, lawyer, accountant, doctor, etc)
- Any special instructions for funeral rites or burial requests
- Family history
- Other relevant documents

COMPLETING THE FORMS

Once your documents are collected and organised, you are ready to begin your planning exercise. In each chapter of this book, you will find insights, opinions and practical tips to develop your own financial plan.

These general observations and insights are provided to help you make decisions and take the actions needed to achieve your own unique personal objectives. The resulting plan for action — your own Wealth Wisdom Plan — is captured in three forms included at the back of this book: an Annual Budget, a Monthly Budget Tracker and a Personal Wealth Schedule.

Annual Budget (Form I)

This form captures the main categories of income and expense. In the income column you can enter your salary, bonus, interest income, dividends and all other sources of income.

You will then need to subtract public pension deductions and income tax to determine your net income.

In the expense columns you should note down all expenses relative to the listed categories, plus any other expenses that do not fall into one of these categories.

You can now calculate the money you will have available for savings and investment by deducting your total expenses from your net income.

While this mathematical calculation is quite correct, there is another way to look at the numbers. Putting the same words in a different order can place the idea in a very different light.

While income minus expenses does equal savings, a much more valuable way to help you meet your financial targets is to consider that *income minus savings equals expenses*.

This simple approach gives you a clear view of the amount of money you can spend while still achieving your savings, investment and personal wealth targets.

Monthly Budget Tracker (Form II)

This form allows you to see how well you are doing against the budgeted annual income and expense figures you have entered on Form I. By checking on progress regularly and making necessary adjustments as you go, you will be in full control of your finances at every step of the way.

It is essential to keep tight control over your budget both to ensure that your plans are realistic and to be sure that you continue to act on those plans into which you have put so much effort.

The reason to keep a regular watch on your budget can be illustrated by the principles of rocket science. It is easy, they tell us, to keep a rocket on course if there are regular checks on progress and any variations from the prescribed trajectory swiftly corrected. This approach requires a large number of small corrections; it saves fuel and reduces, quite dramatically, the risk of the rocket missing its intended objective.

On the other hand, once a rocket strays a long way off course, it is far more difficult and expensive to correct its flight path — and far less likely that the rocket will arrive at its intended destination.

Like a rocket, frequent and small adjustments in your own Wealth Wisdom Plan are a much better approach to hit a target than desperate intervention just short of a disaster.

Personal Wealth Schedule (Form III)

We have already discussed the first two sections of Form III in Chapter 3: Your Wealth Objectives, but in order to complete your Wealth Wisdom Plan you will now need to enter information into the final section of this form, the savings and investment portfolio.

The figures to input here include those for major assets such as your residential and non-residential property, cash and deposits in local and foreign currency, shares, bonds, mutual funds, public and private pensions, commodities, art and antiques, private equity, derivatives and 'other' asset categories (for example, vehicles).

Non-mortgage debts: These assets need then to be adjusted by the total liabilities you possess. For most people, these liabilities are mainly debts and unpaid taxes. The full list of non-mortgage debt will include vehicle loans, consumer finance, credit card debts, unpaid income or capital gains tax, guarantees and other liabilities you have incurred over time.

Your personal wealth, also called your 'net worth', will be the difference between your total assets and total liabilities. Both categories need to be documented and managed wisely if you are to maximise your own net worth over time.

A Total Plan

Like a high-quality corporate report, your Wealth Wisdom Plan is a total approach to address all aspects of your finances.

With the knowledge gained from this book, you will be able to organise your information, account for all sources of income and expense using Forms I and II (your personal profit and loss statement) and link that statement to a full analysis of your assets and liabilities on Form III (your own balance sheet).

Completion and regular revision of these forms and disciplined action to manage your finances in accordance with their content, will support the creation, protection and growth of your own personal wealth over many years.

༜ 5 ༝

CULTURAL ASPECTS
OF PERSONAL FINANCE

Every culture in the world carries with it a whole range of deep influences on the lives of its members. The clothes we wear, the food we eat, the music we listen to, the houses we live in, the holidays we celebrate, the god or gods we worship, the schools we attend, the family structures we adopt and a whole host of other elements of life can be profoundly influenced by the cultures from which we come.

Cultural differences will thus influence very profoundly the content of our Wealth Wisdom Plans and the approach chosen to organise our personal finances.

A few examples of issues which may need to be considered in order to develop a realistic plan to optimise your own wealth creation are set out below.

PSYCHOLOGY OF FAMILY CONTROL

One of the biggest issues arising in the context of financial planning is the psychology of control within a family. The issue, which is common to all cultures, is dealt with in very different ways across the world.

In Japan, many company employees (known in Japanese as *sararimen*) turn over their entire salary to their wives, receiving 10% back in cash for personal spending. The wives take care of all other spending and investment decisions. This is even true in the family of the head of one of Japan's largest stock brokerage companies.

In contrast, women in some countries are deliberately kept in the dark about important financial matters and are only given information about, or control over, the day-to-day household budget. The omnipotent husband or father controls all other expenditure — and all other aspects of family economics — regardless of whether or not the women of the family are more capable of planning, earning, spending or investing money.

Among most modern, educated couples and families a model has emerged which is common across Asian and Western cultures. In this model both the male and female partner contribute to the development and monitoring of a financial plan, each giving in accordance with his or her different abilities.

RELIGIOUS CONSIDERATIONS

Some religions require that a specific amount of money be set aside as a contribution to the community every year, or encourage gifts to the poor and needy. In all cases, religiously inspired principles, financial obligations and voluntary donations need to be taken into account when planning for the future.

ISLAMIC PRINCIPLES

Some religions, notably Islam, set out principles which need to be taken into account in all phases of financial planning and investment. This has led to the development of specific products for Islamic banking, including Islamic savings products, investment products and home mortgages.

Islamic principles with regard to a *Haj* pilgrimage, wills, charity, equal treatment of children and wives, and other elements of life with financial consequences will also need to be taken into account in the development of a full financial plan for individuals and families of this faith.

MULTI-GENERATIONAL FAMILY CONTRIBUTIONS

In many Eastern cultures, the multi-generational family plays a much more important role than it does in Western civilizations. Taking care of parents can be as important a part of the plan as taking care of children. Where this is the case, the implications need to be taken fully into account in your Wealth Wisdom Plan.

NATIONALITY DIFFERENCES

In addition to the cultural differences of religion, family pattern and historic identity, nationality can play an important role in your planning exercise in other ways. For example,

Singaporeans need to consider the financial consequences of the CPF, Malaysians the EPF and Americans the Social Security system and the implications of worldwide taxation.

It is essential that the approach you take when drawing up your Wealth Wisdom Plan reflects the unique cultural aspects of your own situation, while still allowing you to employ the best global approach to personal financial management.

Part II

INCOME AND EXPENDITURE

⊙ 6 ⊙

THE BUDGET PROCESS

Whether it has been consciously designed or not, almost everyone has to operate within a financial budget.

We have income and expenses (often limited by our income). We have bank accounts, make pension contributions, pay insurance premiums and make investments. All of these activities take place within some kind of framework.

The ways we organise our financial lives vary enormously. Individual approaches can be very organised, detailed and fully documented; other approaches can be entirely chaotic and undocumented.

WHY BUDGET?

No matter how rich or poor we are, we all live within limited means. We have a limited amount of income which, in turn, limits our expenditure, savings and investment opportunities.

By taking the time and effort to set and maintain a budget, we can ensure that we get the best result from the money that we have.

Budgeting enables you to focus your resources to achieve goals that can have real impact on your life. This can include buying a house, providing for school fees, travelling abroad or providing insurance for your family in case something goes wrong.

The very down-to-earth discipline of creating and maintaining a budget can help you to achieve tomorrow those things that you can only dream about today.

How Complicated is Budgeting?

As the forms included with this book demonstrate, creating and tracking a budget is very straightforward: INSEAD professor Sarah Mavrinac also points out that there is no need for complex calculations. Doing a budget only requires pulling together information you already have, organising it enough to be able to fill out the three forms which make up your Wealth Wisdom Plan and then using that plan to understand how best to spend, save or invest your money as you go forward.

A good budget shows you where your limits are and how to work within those limits. As if you were making a car journey, budgeting will tell you where you are going, will set out an efficient route to get there, tell you how fast you can drive to get to your destination and which potholes and danger zones should be avoided on the way.

Once your budget is established, you can look beyond it to see how your income can be enhanced, how your expenses could be better regulated and what you should be doing with your savings and investment money.

How often should I do a Budget?

Most people do an annual budget, often at the beginning of the year, with a significant review in between only if there is a major life change such as a job change, marriage, divorce, birth, property purchase or other major change in lifestyle or location. In the absence of such an event, we would recommend that you, too, prepare a budget once a year.

How and when should I Get Started?

There is no better time to start than the present. The sooner you start, the sooner you will finish your Wealth Wisdom Plan and begin to benefit from an improved approach to financial management.

You can and should pace yourself through the exercise. What matters most is the quality of results you achieve, not the speed at which you complete the forms. After a section, or after a few sections, take a brief break, clear your mind, note your progress and return to the form — maybe even the next day — when you are ready to take on the next challenge with renewed vigour.

Like a long car journey, taking breaks along the way can make the whole trip far more pleasant.

Tracking Progress

Now that the purpose and method for budgeting have been set out, you can establish monthly checkpoints and monitor progress against your own Wealth Wisdom Plan objectives and targets.

In order to track your progress, making sure that your trajectory does not err too far from your intended target, your Wealth Wisdom Plan should include completion of the Monthly Budget Tracker form included with this book (Form II).

Your budget will only have value if it is tracked and maintained throughout the year. The effort you have invested in the planning process means you are far more likely to start on the right track, but only a firm resolution to stay on course will allow you to get the full benefits of your efforts.

SMALL INVESTMENT, BIG PAYBACK

By using this simple control device, essentially just an income and expense monitor to be reviewed quickly on a monthly basis, you may be much more in control of your expenses than before.

Doing a budget and controlling your finances means you are doing the best for your family, acting in a responsible way and perhaps showing your family and children how to be responsible as well.

Budgeting is only a small investment of time, but can offer a great payback in many areas, not the least of which is the knowledge that you are fully aware and firmly in control of your own financial destiny.

❦ 7 ❦

INCOME EXPECTATIONS AND CAREER MANAGEMENT

Some fortunate individuals inherit vast sums of unearned capital but, for most of us, our regular salaries are the main source of our livelihood and the origins of our wealth. In some families, dual incomes provide a greater source of funds for savings and investment.

Having the right approach to your job and your career — which are two different things — can make all the difference in the level of wealth you create and the level of personal satisfaction you enjoy.

Your job is the employment in which you are currently engaged. Your career is the collection of jobs in which you are engaged over your entire working life.

Know for Whom and Why You Work

The first principle of any career strategy is to be clear about who is responsible for your career. You are.

Andrew Carnegie, one of the greatest entrepreneurs in the history of the world, once said: "Anyone who thinks he works for someone else is making a big mistake".

No matter at what level in the organisation you find yourself, or who owns the business or organisation in which you are employed, when it boils down to it, you are always working for yourself and your family.

You work to provide the necessities of life: a roof over your head, food on the table, clothes on your back, an education for your children and medical care for those you love. You work for the present, but also for the future. None of us wants to be destitute or a burden to our family in our old age. These 'need-to-haves' are our first priority.

But as well as the 'need-to-haves,' we also work to provide the 'nice-to-have' items that make our lives easier, more beautiful, more pleasant or more glamorous.

There can also be an important element of generosity in what we do professionally; we can work to provide funds for charity, to help those less well-off than we are. In considering the deeper reasons for our efforts, we can also find a sense of higher purpose and accomplishment for ourselves as individuals in the jobs we currently hold.

Give Your Best to Your Current Job Every Day

Sometimes, it is all too easy for us to underestimate the value of our current employment. To understand just how important it is, imagine how we would feel — and what we would do — if the same awful thing that has happened to millions of hardworking people around the world happened to us. Imagine, just for a moment, what life would be like if you lost your job tomorrow.

Unfortunately, this could become a reality far more easily than we might think. In today's world, there is no such thing as a job for life. There is no longer a guarantee in any organisation in any country that the job we have today will be there in a year's time.

Companies suffer relentless pressure from competition, globalisation and capital markets to become more efficient every year. Companies in the manufacturing and service sector may move their operations to remote locations, and even to foreign countries, in their search for lower operating costs and more attractive markets. Outsourcing and subcontracting are constant threats to employment in many companies.

Even governments are under pressure to control spending and reduce costs, to outsource functions to the private sector and to become more effective and more efficient.

Within companies, there is competition for advancement and responsibility from younger and less expensive colleagues.

None of these pressures will reduce in the coming years; if anything they are more likely to increase significantly. Given this scary scenario and given the desire almost all of us have to do the best we can, it is extremely important to value our jobs each and every day. This means:

- Focusing on the results you achieve.
- Maximising the value you create.
- Contributing to a harmonious work environment.
- Developing the people who work for you.
- Providing honest views on areas for improvement.
- Putting your full weight behind the achievement of goals set for yourself, your colleagues, your department and your organisation as a whole.

Whether you are the president of the company or the newest employee in the mail room, the value you can contribute should be as great as you can possibly make it.

There are three reasons for this:

- By performing to the best of your ability, you will benefit from a feeling of personal fulfilment and growth you would not otherwise find.
- You will maximise the potential in your current employment – higher pay, faster promotions, more responsibility and greater recognition.
- You will increase your options and value in the job market.

INVEST IN YOURSELF

Optimising your current job and career path does not happen randomly. Moving forward and upward in our professional lives requires hard work, a constant focus on the results we achieve, the development of new skills and taking full advantage of the opportunities presented within and from outside our current jobs.

You can invest in your job and career through attending training courses, reading at home, attending lectures, obtaining a part-time degree or certificate and through other areas of formal and informal career development. Find out from bosses, HR departments and colleagues how you could benefit from training and development opportunities already existing within your organisation.

MAXIMISE LIFETIME INCOME

Most people focus their career planning on how to maximise their income and bonus for this year and, perhaps, the next. A more thoughtful approach encourages us to maximise lifetime career earnings, not just next year's salary and bonus. This requires a long-term view. It may also require a big change from one year to the next. Maximising lifetime income may also lead us to step down from a job altogether, invest in obtaining a new skill or credential and then re-enter the job market at a higher level.

SEEK OUT MENTORS

Even though we are responsible for our own career development, none of us can claim full and individual credit for our successes. Other people count. Bosses and colleagues can be instrumental in our advances.

In addition to working well with and consulting those in our immediate sphere of contact at work, it can also be useful to enlist the help of one or two friends or advisers outside our organisations. Mentors, in the form of career guides, personal advisers and people to whom we can turn in times of difficulty, have an important role to play.

It is often very difficult to see our own strengths and weaknesses. Most people overestimate their abilities and may be blind to some significant weaknesses; others may be unable to see their own strengths, and hence discount their own accomplishments and underestimate their capabilities.

In both cases, seeking out the advice and counsel of someone who will take an honest and intelligent interest in your affairs can help enormously.

EXPLORE ALTERNATIVE CAREER OPPORTUNITIES

It is important to keep your career options open and everyone should have a Plan B in mind in case of lay-off or other unexpected terminations of employment, or simply to make sure they are not missing out on advantageous and more attractive alternatives which might be available in the job market.

Whatever your circumstances, the importance of salary and bonus to your wealth plans means you should manage the risk and the opportunity of alternative job prospects with great care and attention.

THE 'S'-CURVE

Davy Lau, a partner at the international executive search firm Egon Zehnder International and a key proponent of a career strategy to maximise lifetime income, describes a successful career as a series of S-shaped curves. At the beginning of every new job, even within the same company, there is a slow, initial phase as you 'get to know the ropes'. This is followed by a very powerful phase of growth, development and new accomplishment. This phase can last for many years, or for a far shorter period of time.

At some point though, a job becomes more routine; the pace of learning and development slows down; the job can feel repetitive and monotonous. When you hit this plateau, it is probably time to look for new challenges — preferably within the same company, but perhaps within a new organisation. You then start again at the beginning stages of another exciting S-curve opportunity.

HAVE A CAREER STRATEGY

Ironically, despite its importance in wealth creation, few people have a career strategy. For some, a job is seen as a big chore to be endured for the sake of a regular pay cheque. Not only does this negative attitude dangerously increase the risk of losing a job, it also seriously reduces anyone's sense of personal achievement.

A successful career consists of more than a pay cheque. Professional accomplishment, respect, learning, teaching and mentoring others, attending to new and interesting tasks, gaining more responsibility, meeting and working with interesting people can define 'success' in different ways and contribute to the creation of a successful career.

Every strategy has a vision, a set of goals, a timetable, responsibilities and checkpoints along the way. Every career deserves a strategy, and the best strategic goal in career management is to maximise lifetime income, not just your next salary cheque.

In every career strategy you should set short-term goals for your current job and longer term goals for your career. Davy Lau also points out the value of doing the 'Funeral Exercise' to help you plan a meaningful career: Imagine you can see your own funeral. What would you like people to say about you and your life? From the answers to these questions, you can plan your career strategy and see what steps are necessary to progress along the right lines.

BE READY FOR THE UNEXPECTED

Given the volatility of the business environment today, we can no longer plan on life-long employment with a company the way our parents did. We must be prepared for the unexpected — both the good and the bad.

Getting through difficult times can be a blessing. Our best experiences usually confirm what we already know. It is our worst experiences which teach us the most. But no matter in which circumstances we find ourselves, a positive attitude is a great companion. As Davy Lau puts it: "A positive attitude is the fuel for success."

By paying attention to the career principles set out above and by having a Wealth Wisdom Plan with a contingency element built in, you can be as ready as possible for whatever comes your way.

How do I Get Started?

Although the perspectives provided above may have you thinking differently about your career, it is essential that you enter the most current information on your existing income expectations in your Wealth Wisdom Plan.

On the first line of your Annual Budget you enter your current income. Also note down any other income you might be fortunate enough to receive. Many people make the mistake of adding in speculative income — income they hope to have but which may never materialise — and then build a spending pattern to match this inflated figure. It is all too easy to spend money we do not yet have — and may never receive. Your budget should be based on realistic estimates rather than hope.

Once your income is entered, you need to subtract two items to arrive at an appropriate net income figure. The first item is public pension deductions, the second is income tax. In Chapter 8 we will address the issue of taxes, an important part of any budget, in more detail.

This leaves you with your net income — the income available for expenditure or saving and investing.

Income	
Salary and Bonus	
Other Income	
(*minus* Public Pension Deductions)	
(*minus* Income Tax)	
Net Income	

Your next step is to set out where you plan to spend your money during the year.

Although each plan is as unique as the individual putting it together, it may be useful to have some indication of what professional advisers agree on as useful benchmarks.

Financial expert Juliana Ng provides some basic ratios that can serve as a starting point for your own consideration when she says that your savings rate should be at least 10% of your income and that, for debt management, the total of your debt repayments (including mortgage payments) should not exceed 35% of your take-home income.

∞ 8 ∞

TAXES

Nothing is sure but death and taxes.

Any good financial plan needs to address these two issues clearly, just as it addresses the less certain elements of our lives.

In almost all wealth management plans, taxes are a major expense item and need to be taken into account for investment strategy, estate planning and income and expense management.

Managing your taxes effectively may save you an enormous amount of money and accelerate your wealth development plans significantly.

In Chapter 7, income tax was included in the steps leading up to the calculation of your net income. Income tax, however, is not the only tax obligation which needs to be taken into consideration when optimising your approach to wealth management.

Value-added taxes, in the form of GST or sales tax, have crept into the tax systems of many countries and may be present at different levels in individual states within the same country. In the USA, for example, the state sales tax is different from state to state; in Australia it is a national 10%.

Other taxes such as petrol tax, import tax, vehicle tax, road tax, car radio tax, wealth tax, capital gains tax and inheritance tax can also play a role in our spending patterns and estate plans.

ACTIVE MANAGEMENT IS ESSENTIAL

While the existence of taxation may be a certainty, the impact of taxes on your wealth creation plans can vary substantially. Not only is it important to understand the sources and rules of taxation, it is also essential to understand how we can legally reduce those taxes to the lowest level possible.

In all cases it makes sense to take a few basic steps to ensure you are not paying more tax than is necessary:

Know the rules: Tax policies change, often on an annual basis, as governments set their own budget for the year. It is important to be aware of current tax laws in your country to know what options you have to reduce or avoid your tax burden. The bad news is that the tax code in most countries is long and complicated; in the USA it is 70,000 pages long.

The best way to find out about taxes is to speak to a professional financial planner, accountant or specialist tax adviser. In addition, there are also many commercial guides available in bookstores and websites specific to each country which are available at low cost, or even for free. These sources can provide a basic understanding of tax policies, including applicable tax rates, possible deductions and other relevant information.

Make the most of available deductions: Although it is not necessary to know the whole code, it is important to know which deductions you can take as they may reduce your overall tax burden. In some countries, deductions are allowable for mortgage payments, educational expenses and selected pension contributions.

Some taxes can be reduced by taking into account the tax element of every major purchase you make. Some can be reduced by shopping in duty-free zones, avoiding peak-hour road charges, purchasing a smaller vehicle or establishing trusts to avoid estate duties where possible.

Use corporate or trust structures where applicable: Although more useful for the high end of the tax-paying population, the use of a corporate or trust structure, particularly for individuals with high net worth and an international lifestyle, can be an important part of tax management.

Plan for the inevitable: Even if we sometimes feel immortal, planning to reduce inheritance tax can be an important part of an estate plan. Although some countries have relatively low rates of inheritance tax, there may be ways to reduce even that small burden by, for example, increasing the proportion of your assets captured in a property used as a main residence (tax free up to S$9 million in Singapore) instead of holding assets of the same value in cash, which attract estate duty.

Other countries have high estate duties with varying exemptions. The conditions prevailing in the country where you are domiciled (i.e. where your estate will be taxed) might make different approaches more, or less, attractive.

Stay within the law: Sometimes it may be tempting to slip into the 'black' economy and evade, by deceit or non-declaration, taxes which you have a legal obligation to pay. As in all other aspects of life, ensuring that you stay on the right side of the law is essential for both moral and practical reasons. Penalties can be high and may, under certain circumstances, even result in a jail term as well as a financial penalty.

Take Full Advantage of Benefits

Taxes play an important role in wealth redistribution by taking greater sums of money from the wealthy to provide benefits and services which are available to everyone at a lower cost — or even on a cost-free basis.

To this end, you can manage your tax for maximum personal benefit in an indirect way by making sure that you take full advantage of the benefits and services for which you are already paying. Use community centres, public libraries, transport systems, national health services and the state education system wherever possible.

Nobody likes paying taxes but, by taking full advantage of the benefits that your taxes provide, you may, at the very least, reduce your stress at tax-return time.

Types of Tax

It is worthwhile having a closer look at a few of the major taxes we pay to understand how we could better manage them:

Income tax

Whether your income is earned (i.e. salary and bonus) or passive (e.g. rental income, royalties or licensing fees you might receive), it will be subject to tax in most jurisdictions.

Income tax is usually progressive, which means it is payable at a rate which rises with the level of income. The tax rate on lower income is substantially less than the tax rate on higher incomes. In Singapore, for example, the highest tax rate payable is now 21%, while for lower incomes no tax, or a very low tax rate, is payable.

In some European countries the highest tax rate can be between 40% and 60%. In the USA the highest income tax rate payable is now 35% on a national level plus any income tax the relevant state may levy, while in Malaysia the highest rate is 28%. In Hong Kong, the highest income tax rate is 16%.

Worldwide tax policy: Some countries, such as the USA, have a worldwide tax policy. No matter where you live, and no matter for how long you have been abroad, anyone holding a US passport or Green Card essentially has to pay US taxes as if he or she were living in the USA.

Multiple jurisdictions: If your income is generated or received in more than one country, more than one tax law may apply. Be sure to check for double taxation agreements to avoid paying too much tax.

Deductibles: There are a number of deductibles available in all tax systems. These deductibles (e.g. expenses which are due to your job or payments to charity) can lower the basis on which the tax is calculated.

Joint filing of income tax: The most advantageous filing approach — separate or joint — varies by country. As part of the process of understanding the relevant tax laws, it is important that you understand the tax implications of each option. An expert adviser may come up with some novel ways to reduce taxes with little effort. For example, balancing salaries and filing separately may reduce a couple's tax burden as opposed to filing jointly and having to pay a higher tax rate.

VAT/GST/Sales tax

While most of us are exposed to sales tax on a daily basis, either as VAT or as GST, there are ways to reduce this tax item in your personal financial planning.

Take, for example, goods bought during a holiday abroad. VAT, GST or other sales tax levied in the country of purchase can often be claimed back if the amount paid for the goods is above a certain threshold. If you go on a holiday to Europe and purchase something for which a VAT of 17.5% is levied, as is the case for Great Britain, you can claim the VAT back, minus some charges payable to the GST Refund processing entity. This rebate may be for an amount of money not bargained for initially and can come as a nice surprise as you leave a high-tax country. Even upon declaring your goods to customs authorities as you return home to a lower tax country, you may have received a significant net tax savings by your actions.

Product specific taxes

There are product specific taxes which are also necessary to consider as they may affect both your tax position and your purchase decisions.

One such example is petrol tax, which is included in the price you pay to fill up your tank. If this tax is raised, the overall price for petrol increases, perhaps making it necessary to adjust your budget for transportation.

Other examples are alcohol and tobacco tax, known as 'sin taxes' in the USA. These taxes can be high and make duty-free purchase opportunities well worth taking if you consume any of these items.

In some countries, luxury goods taxes are payable on goods not considered essential, such as high-end cars, perfumes, expensive watches and designer leather goods.

Road tax

Many countries, including Singapore and Malaysia, levy a road tax on vehicles registered in these countries. It can be paid either biannually or annually and is based on the engine capacity and type, i.e. if the vehicle has a diesel or ordinary petrol-engine. In the future, other engine types, such as hybrid engines, might attract reductions.

Obviously, those seeking to pay less tax should consider the size and type of the vehicle they purchase.

Capital gains tax

Capital gains tax is the tax levied on a 'capital gain', i.e. the difference between what you paid for an item and the price at which it is sold. As with income tax, capital gains tax will vary from country to country.

Although countries such as Singapore and Hong Kong do not have capital gains tax, this tax can be highly relevant in other countries in which you may consider investment.

For example, some countries exempt from tax the gains of a sale of your primary residence (e.g. the UK) and others do not (e.g. the USA).

Property tax

Property tax can be levied upon real estate owned. Property tax may be, for example, levied in the USA, Canada, Europe, Malaysia, Hong Kong, and Australia. This tax is dealt with in more detail in Chapter 19: Property.

Wealth tax

Although the USA, UK and Singapore do not have a wealth tax, this tax can be relevant in other countries in Europe and

Asia. A wealth tax is calculated from an individual's net worth and is usually paid annually.

There are many legal ways to reduce a wealth tax by intelligent financial planning. Some Europeans, for example, borrow heavily in a wealth tax country in which they have a house in order to reduce their exposed wealth, even if they do not need a mortgage at all.

Inheritance tax

Inheritance tax (estate duty) is levied in many countries, although the threshold above which it is due and the rates applied vary considerably from one country to another. Estate duty calculations are based upon everything a person owns, minus any debts, at the time of death. It is levied upon the heirs of the deceased's estate.

Some countries such as Malaysia, India, Canada, New Zealand and Australia do not have inheritance tax. Hong Kong only levies inheritance tax on assets situated in Hong Kong. The UK, however, has quite substantial inheritance tax, as does the USA. Singapore levies inheritance tax but at a relatively lower percentage and with a relatively higher threshold.

For more information on inheritance tax and estate planning, please refer to Chapter 37.

UNDERSTAND BEFORE YOU ACT

As you can see from the above examples, types and rates of taxes vary considerably from country to country and can have a big impact on your personal finances if your career, spending habits or investments involve more than one country. If this is the case for you, or will be the case at a later date, you should consult a tax adviser for advice about your personal tax situation. As tax professional Wu Soo Mee points out, it is important to know the tax law of every country where you receive income or where you may encounter a tax obligation.

It is important not only to budget for taxes under the current rules, but also to stay abreast of changes in the tax law. This does not mean you are expected to be a tax expert, but it can pay off to know the tax basics as they apply to your own situation and wealth plans.

Ignorance is no excuse for paying too little — or too much — tax.

❦ 9 ❧

EXPENSES

Amusing or distressing, a review of how we actually spend our money is an activity through which we will find out a lot about ourselves. Our spending patterns may be one of the best indicators of our values, our priorities and our real life choices.

Not all of our spending patterns are going to be obvious; by going over credit card and bank statements you may be surprised to see where you are actually spending your money.

ENSURE ALL COSTS CAPTURED

One of the classic errors we make in budgeting for expenses is to fail to capture all items of expenditure. If we are not comprehensive in capturing all cost items and allocating them properly, we will be trying to build a robust budget on a weak foundation.

Without the certainty that all costs have been captured you will not be able to come to an intelligent view as to whether your expenditure is too high, just right or even too low.

A breakdown of core categories is listed below to help you capture all of your own expenses. The best way to approach each category may be to write down *regular* monthly expenses such as payments for housing (rent or mortgage), electricity, water, gas, oil (for heating purposes in colder countries), telephone and education, then focus on irregular payments which may be paid only once a year, such as building insurance.

HOUSING

For most people, housing costs takes up a significant portion of their available budget. Make sure you capture all housing related expenses including, for example, payments for pest control and gardening (these costs can be entered in the 'other' category). More information on mortgages can be found in Chapter 11.

Housing	
Rent	
Mortgage	
Electricity	
Water	
Gas	
Repairs and Maintenance	
Other	
Total Housing	

Transportation

Transportation is another major expense category. Do you have a car? More than one car? Is it paid for in full or do you service a car loan? In this category, it is necessary to include insurance and all operating costs for the car as well as any associated taxes. Further, the cost for parking, petrol and repairs has to be taken into account as well as taxi fares and public transport charges you might incur.

This area may be the second largest area of expense for some people, especially in parts of Asia where cars can be two to three times as expensive as they are in Europe or the USA. See Chapter 12: Transportation and Vehicle Purchase for more information.

Transportation	
Car Loan (principal only)	
Insurance	
Road Tax	
ERP	
Petrol	
Parking	
Repairs	
Taxi	
Public Transport	
Other	
Total Transportation	

TELEPHONE AND INTERNET

With new offers and special deals becoming available every day, managing our communications costs is more challenging but potentially more rewarding now than in the past.

Often a source of uncontrolled expense, mobile phone charges, in particular, should be carefully reviewed, whether settled by pre-paid card or by a set contract.

Switching to a VoIP (Voice over Internet Protocol) service such as Skype can reduce your call charges enormously.

Telephone and Internet	
Telephone	
Internet	
Equipment	
Other	
Total Telephone & Internet	

CREDIT CARD AND LOAN FEES AND INTEREST

One category of hidden — but possibly major — costs is loan fees and interest payments on credit cards and consumer finance (appliances, electronics, furniture, etc.). Chapter 13: Credit Cards and Consumer Finance, deals with this subject in more detail.

It is important here to separate the cost of the items purchased — for example airline tickets (which should be entered as a vacation expense) from the financial charges associated with such a purchase. This area of financial services costs should only capture fees and interest paid on all credit cards and other loans, along with overdraft penalties and bank handling charges.

You may be surprised how these hidden charges build up to a significant sum — and make an easy target for reduction.

Fees and Interest on Credit Cards and Loans	
Credit Card Fees	
Credit Card Interest	
Other Loan Fees	
Other Loan Interest	
Other Fees and Charges	
Total Fees and Interest on Credit Cards and Loans	

INSURANCE

Insurance expenses (premiums) can come in either regular or irregular payments. For more details on insurance-related issues please refer to Chapter 10.

Insurance	
House Insurance	
Content Insurance	
Health Insurance	
Life Insurance	
Disability Insurance	
Travel Insurance	
Other	
Total Insurance	

MEDICAL CARE

Many people overlook budgeting for medical costs which will not be reimbursed by medical insurance.

Medical Care	
Medical Care	
minus expenses to be reimbursed by insurance	

GROCERIES AND RESTAURANTS

No matter if you eat in or out, all expenses incurred for food should be noted down. Expenses for wine and other alcoholic beverages should also be captured in this category (or, alternatively, as an entertainment expense).

Food (groceries and restaurants)	
Groceries	
Eating Out	
Wine, Beer and Spirits	
Other	
Total Food	

EDUCATION

Payments for education and school-related activities come into this category. It is important to capture all expenses such as school fees, transportation, school-related activities, co-curricular activities, extra tuition and other similar expenses. If you pay into a plan for future educational needs for your children, this should come out of the figure entered for 'Available for Savings and Investments'. Only current education-related expenses should be listed here. Chapter 14 deals with Educational Finance in more detail.

Education	
School Fees	
Transportation	
School-related Activities	
CCA 1	
CCA 2	
CCA 3	
Tuition	
Other	
Total Education	

PERSONAL EXPENSES

The next category of items relates to personal expenses, including clothing, hair care, tobacco, movies, books and other entertainment expenses, hobbies and other items not captured above.

Again, there are 'must-haves', 'nice-to-haves', and, in some cases, 'bad-to-haves'. Target the 'bad-to-haves' for reduction first, and then, if necessary, some of the lower priority 'nice-to-haves'. As a pure matter of fact, the annual cost of smoking one packet of cigarettes per day in Singapore — not taking into account increased health care and insurance costs — amounts to more than S$4,000 per year!

Personal Expenses	
Clothing	
Entertainment	
Club Memberships	
Books, Magazines	
Hair Care	
Tobacco	
Hobbies	
Other Personal Items	
Total Personal Expenses	

Vacations

A further category deals with vacations and vacation-related travel. These expenses can be significant and, being irregular payments, easily forgotten as part of an annual budget plan.

Vacations	
Travel	
Accommodation	
Car Rental	
Extra Out-of-pocket Expenses	
Other	
Total Vacations	

CHARITY

Many well-meaning individuals give to charity every year. This expense can take the form of a regular donation or a once-a-year contribution. However you give, it is important to account for your generosity in advance. Charity and philanthropy are addressed in more detail in Chapter 15.

Charity	
Charity 1	
Charity 2	
Other	
Total Charity	

GIFTS

Gifts are often overlooked as expense items. However, from birthday to Christmas presents, from '*hong bao*', small red and gold envelopes containing cash gifts and intended to bring a year of prosperity to wedding presents, they all need to be budgeted for.

Gifts	
Birthday Gifts	
Christmas Gifts	
New Year Gifts	
Special Occasion Gifts	
Other Gifts	
Total Gifts	

DOMESTIC HELP

For families lucky enough to be able to engage domestic help, another category to include in expense budgets is your maid's salary and associated costs such as insurance, home leave, levy (in Singapore), medical care, living expenses and other related items.

Domestic Help	
Salary	
Levy	
Medical Fees	
Home Leave	
Other	
Total Domestic Help	

CONTINGENCY

As one great philosopher said, "Life is more like a wrestling match than a choreographed dance." Since we never know what unexpected events can upset our plans, it is best to set aside a certain amount for unknown costs. See Chapter 31: Planning for the Unexpected, for more information on contingency planning.

Contingency	

OTHER EXPENSES

Within any normal year, most of us are likely to incur one-off expenses which may be large (for example new pieces of furniture) or small (general miscellaneous items). This category should anticipate these items so that your overall expense allocation is as comprehensive as possible.

Other Expenses	

PRINCIPLES OF REVIEW

Once all of these individual categories are properly defined, itemised and budgeted for, they can serve as useful checklists to help review your overall level of spending.

Key questions to ask yourself for each category and sub-category of expense include:

- Which items in this category are 'need-to-haves'?
- Which items in this category are 'nice-to-haves'?
- Which items in this category are 'bad-to-haves' but part of life?
- Is my expenditure in this category too high?
- In which areas should/could the level of expenditure be decreased? Increased?
- Am I spending well?
- Have I shopped around enough?
- What are the alternatives?
- If this is a 'whole family' plan, who will be responsible for which items of expense?

A Family Affair

Documenting the past and setting a future expense budget does not need to be an individual effort. Many expenses are incurred on behalf of the whole family and their documentation and forecasting can be treated openly as an opportunity to share understanding and responsibility.

If you are uncertain about which children should be involved and at what age, you may want to do your budget alone at first and then go through appropriate categories with other members of the family. You may get useful thoughts and inputs from everyone, including children and parents. In this way, evaluating your expenses will not only reflect how you deal with money, but also how well you deal with the life-skills education of your family.

Children of sufficient maturity should also learn that life has its ups and downs financially, emotionally, and in every other aspect; change will take place and everyone will need to adapt.

Less Physical Nature of Money

Today, children usually do not see as many cash transactions as was the case even a few years ago. Credit card charges, Internet banking, direct debits, cheque payments and other virtual transactions have taken the place of cash as a way to buy and sell things.

In the absence of seeing cash in use, planning and evaluating your expenditure can give older children more financial awareness and highlight the need for intelligent management of both expenses and overall family finance.

❧ 10 ☙

INSURANCE

Many people view insurance policies as protection against worst-case scenarios. Others may see them as protectors of assets, incomes and private wealth from loss, damage or liability from litigation. But insurance can also play an important role as an active method of investment, possibly providing both capital growth and future income. It also has a very important role to play in retirement and estate planning.

Specific goals, such as your children's education, can be pursued through the payments received from a life endowment plan, or ensured in the event of the death of a parent by a term or whole life policy.

TYPES OF INSURANCE

There are many different risks against which we can insure ourselves. We can purchase life insurance, health insurance, car insurance, building insurance, home content insurance, travel insurance and even disaster insurance of all kinds. The main types of insurance are explained below:

Life insurance: There are two broad categories of life insurance: term and whole life. There are two options under each of these two categories: with and without investment.

Whole life policies last from the moment of purchase until the death of the policyholder. Term life policies, as the name suggests, last for a certain term and may terminate well before the death of the policyholder. For example, a parent may want to take out a term life policy until his children are through with their graduate schooling, a date which can be as late as 27-years-old. By taking out a simple term life policy (without investment) with a death or incapacitation benefit, a parent can ensure an educational future for his or her child, even if the parent dies or becomes incapacitated before the child's schooling is complete.

Both whole life and term life policies can provide for death benefit only, or can have an investment component added. The addition of an investment element in which the insurance company receives and invests funds on your behalf as well as insuring against your death or incapacitation can be an easy way for an unsophisticated investor to build a nest egg for the future. Term life, without investment, is the cheapest type of life policy. Whole life, with investment, is the most expensive.

If you choose a life policy with an investment element included, it will not only pay death benefit if you die within the term of the insurance, but may also pay a considerable sum if you out-live the insurance period.

Selecting this type of policy allows an unsophisticated investor to outsource his or her investment needs to a professional insurance investor. However, be warned: costs for this service can be high, and returns from this type of insurance may be relatively low. All the same, this may be a low risk avenue worth pursuing as part of a balanced portfolio with minimum involvement on the part of the individual policy holder/investor.

Some insurance experts recommend that insurance investment policies be used by less sophisticated investors with less than S$150,000 available capital to invest.

Life insurance policies, with their legal jargon and terminology can be difficult to understand. If you already have life insurance, read the policy carefully and review it against your answers to the important questions listed below.

If you are shopping for life insurance, make sure you choose the right policy or policies to meet your personal objectives. Ask your insurance adviser to go through the following questions with you:

- Should I be looking for whole life insurance or term life insurance? If term life insurance is more appropriate, how long should coverage last? At which level?
- What benefit will be paid in case of death?
- Does the policy pay incapacitation benefits?
- Who is the beneficiary in the case of death of the policyholder? Is this the right person or is a change necessary? (This is important if the policyholder got married, divorced, remarried or had a child since he or she last reviewed the policy.)
- What are my monthly or yearly premium payments?
- Should I review the amount for which I am insured?
- How highly rated is the insurance company issuing the policy?
- Am I able to convert the policy from a death-benefit-only policy to one which will also pay me an annuity?
- Does my policy have a surrender value? If so, what is it?
- If the policy has an investment element, what are the terms of the investment?
- Are my insurance policies in line with my overall wealth management objectives?

- Are there any other clauses in the policy which are of particular relevance to me personally?

It may be worth noting that some amendments to existing policies will cost money and rates and terms will vary from one provider to another. It would be worthwhile to speak to at least two insurance agents or financial planners to make sure you are getting the most appropriate policy at the best possible price.

Health and dental insurance: The importance of this type of insurance can depend upon where you live. In some countries, healthcare costs may be entirely covered by the state. Private health insurance is therefore not required by the majority of people. This is the case in many European countries. In other countries, private health insurance is necessary to ensure adequate treatment in the case of severe illnesses as public healthcare may be inadequate or not available at reasonable price and within a reasonable time.

Disability insurance: Disability insurance ensures that a person incapacitated and unable to work will still have some income. With this insurance you can, for example, protect your family should you become disabled but still live for many years without being able to provide income as before.

Vehicle insurance: Every registered vehicle is required to have insurance before being driven on the road. This is to protect yourself and others in case of an accident.

When reviewing your vehicle insurance policy, be aware that a good past record (i.e. no previous insurance claims) is reflected in a 'NCD', or no claims discount of up to 70%.

Vehicle insurance rates vary according to type of vehicle, age of registered drivers, location of primary residence of owner, primary use (commercial or personal) mileage driven and other relevant information.

The usual time people review their vehicle insurance is when they purchase a new vehicle or when an insurance premium is due for renewal, although a review of all of your insurance providers, as part of your Wealth Wisdom Plan, may also surface opportunities to get a better policy at the same, or even lower, cost.

House (buildings) insurance: Protection against damage to the structure of your property by, for example, fire, wind (storm), and water, in the form of house or buildings insurance, is essential. It is important, once again, to read the policy accurately to ensure that you are covered for all likely eventualities.

The amount of insurance paid out in the event of one of these potential disasters happening to your property is usually based on the insured value of the property, so it is important to check that the value on your policy is up-to-date. Property values or replacement costs may have gone up substantially since you bought your house or apartment.

Home contents insurance: It is especially important to review this type of insurance policy regularly as the value of your possessions can increase over time without your being aware of the total amount at risk. Whenever you purchase an expensive item, you should review your policy to make sure you have sufficient cover. An expensive purchase could include a new computer, TV, music system, living room suite, piece of jewellery or art object. Home contents should be adequately covered against theft, fire, breakage and other claims to give you the degree of protection you need.

Travel insurance: Many holiday and travel packages include basic insurance cover, such as life insurance and holiday cancellation or evacuation insurance. Some may go further and include protection from accrued costs in case you fall ill while on holiday or have to cancel your vacation unexpectedly (there are usually strict limitations in this clause), or have your belongings stolen.

It should be noted that you may not need to purchase this kind of coverage separately if already covered by your credit card supplier.

Other insurance products: There are many other insurance products available for specific risks, from insurance to cover a pianist's hands to weather insurance which protects farmers in the northern hemisphere if their crops are destroyed by, for example, hail.

INSURANCE NEEDS TO FIT YOUR LIFE STAGE

Determining which insurance is right for you depends on your life stage (single or married, young or old, with or without children), your personal profile and your priorities in life. All of these factors will determine the right mix for you.

In Asia, as around the world, the percentage of family income allocated to insurance varies greatly, from a low of 1% in Indonesia to a high of 10% in Japan. The Japanese, like the Swiss, are relatively heavy consumers of insurance products.

As an example, a family of four, with a 37-year-old father, 35-year-old mother and two children aged seven and five, would be at the peak of demand for insurance as a percent of income.

A family like the one described above, perhaps resident in Singapore and earning S$7,000 per month, might consider investing as much as 5% of income in various insurance products.

Of this 5%, perhaps 3% would go to life insurance, 1% to health insurance and 1% to asset protection insurance products, such as home and vehicle insurance.

While it is important to have the right amount of insurance, it is also important to avoid over-insuring and to avoid coverage where not needed.

WHEN SHOULD YOU REVIEW YOUR INSURANCE NEEDS?

Just as your budget changes as your life changes, your insurance needs also change over time and need to be reviewed periodically.

A sensible time to conduct a major review of your insurance requirements is when setting out your first Wealth Wisdom Plan. You should also review insurance needs when doing your Annual Budget. A quick check every year is wise; perhaps more often for certain insurances, such as household contents, if your needs change substantially.

When reviewing insurance needs, it is worth asking yourself a few quick questions:

- What are your objectives? (e.g. Do you want protection or investment? Are you looking for retirement income?)
- What are your needs?
- Do your current policies cover your needs?
- Do you understand your policy options? (e.g. Opt out charges, cancellation fees, surrender value.)
- Have you checked your existing policies carefully? Are you getting good value and insuring for the right risks and benefits?
- Have you shopped for alternatives?
- Have you spoken to the best adviser?

∞ 11 ∞

MORTGAGES

It is said that a man's home is his castle. This is borne out by the fact that, all over the world, people strive to own their own homes.

In Singapore, for example, 90% of the population own the property they live in. In the USA and UK, around two thirds of the population owns the home they live in.

The decision to buy or rent a property depends on personal circumstances such as age, income and stage of life, as well as other market-driven factors. For example, young people will often rent first and buy later; some countries have rent control laws which make it attractive for eligible people to rent at a subsidised level even if they could very well afford to buy.

In other countries, such as Singapore, people tend to prefer buying over renting first homes. Buying a home has been seen in the past as an investment guaranteeing a high return. This tendency, however, is softening. As property prices in parts of Asia have not risen as rapidly as they once did, more people are reported to be looking into renting a home than they were ten years ago.

Few people can afford to buy a property without having to borrow some money. For most people this will mean taking out a mortgage. A mortgage gives you the opportunity to own a house you may not otherwise be able to afford, but a large mortgage also means a large financial burden and a long-term commitment.

Home ownership means a lot more than just paying the mortgage. The full set of expenses: insurance, repair, renovation, taxes and other items, can be a lot more expensive than buyers originally anticipate.

Owning a property is not a risk-free proposition and capital invested in property may not always be a good investment. At some periods in the past, house prices in some markets have collapsed to levels below the value of the outstanding mortgage on the property, creating 'negative equity', or the situation in which, after sale of the property, the owner would need to raise funds in addition to the sale proceeds to pay off the mortgage. Home buyers may subsequently be very emotionally distressed because of the strain on their finances. This highlights the vital importance of careful contingency planning before making any property purchase decision.

What is a Mortgage?

A mortgage uses real estate, or property, to secure a loan. Most commonly the loan is to finance the purchase of the property itself. A mortgage is a big and long-term commitment; if you fail to make the agreed repayments to the mortgage provider, which is usually a bank, insurer or other financial institution, your home may be repossessed and sold to cover the outstanding loan.

Mortgages can have tax benefits in many countries as repayments are usually tax deductible and, as such, decrease the income exposed for the calculation of your income tax.

MORTGAGE PAYMENTS, FEES AND OTHER RELATED COSTS

Listed below are some of the main costs incurred when purchasing a property:

- Down payment of a percentage of the property value.
- Mortgage: capital repayment.
- Mortgage: interest on loan repayment.
- Property valuation report.
- Structural survey report.
- Mortgage arrangement fee (to lender).
- Mortgage broking fee (to broker).
- Early mortgage settlement fee.
- Life insurance premium.
- Estate agency fee.
- Legal fees.
- Land registry fee.
- Stamp duty.
- Removal fees.
- Utilities and telephone connection charges.
- Repairs, renovation and decoration.

INSURANCE REQUIREMENTS

Property ownership also requires that certain types of insurance be in place for the duration of the mortgage or for the entire period of ownership. These include building insurance and even life insurance.

Life insurance guarantees repayment of the mortgage should the mortgage borrower die before the end of the mortgage term. Although not required from a lender's point of view, home contents insurance should also be budgeted for. These insurances are described in more detail in Chapter 10.

LENGTH OF MORTGAGE TERM

You also need to decide for how long you want to be paying your mortgage. Obviously, monthly payments for a mortgage which spans 10 years will be higher than payments for the same value mortgage to be paid off over 20 years. The bank may look carefully at your age before agreeing your mortgage term: The older you get, the shorter the mortgage term might be (and hence the higher the mortgage payments).

TYPES OF MORTGAGE

There are two main types of mortgage: Interest-only mortgages and repayment mortgages. In both cases you will need to decide whether you choose a mortgage with a fixed or a variable rate of interest. If interest rates go up or down and you do not have a fixed-rate mortgage, your payments will also go up and down.

Interest-only mortgage: With this type of mortgage, your monthly repayments only cover the interest on the loan and not any of the capital costs. Initial mortgage repayments on an interest-only mortgage are relatively low as they do not include capital payments. You may want to pay into an investment, savings or insurance scheme to build up enough money to repay the capital cost of the property at the end of the mortgage term.

Repayment mortgage: This type of mortgage guarantees that the property will be entirely yours at the end of the mortgage term so long as you maintain the payments.

These payments include both capital and interest payments from the start, and are higher than interest-only payments for a similar sized mortgage (at the outset).

REFINANCING A MORTGAGE

Experts tell us it takes effort to make sure you have the best deal on a mortgage for your home. You should frequently shop around for the best deal — not just when you purchase your home or investment property — as other lenders might be offering better value. It might also make sense to refinance more than once, paying back one mortgage and replacing it with a more attractive alternative.

When considering this option, however, a mortgage borrower always needs to keep in mind that refinancing will incur additional charges and fees and can become very costly, if not fully understood throughout the process.

Another reason for refinancing a mortgage, or taking on a different sort of mortgage upon the purchase of a property, might be that a mortgage in an alternative currency becomes more attractive. This may be, for example, because of lower interest rates associated with that currency. For years, low interest rates charged on Yen loans of all kinds have made it an attractive option for mortgage borrowers in Europe.

Very careful consideration is necessary in a mismatched mortgage (a mortgage which is in a different currency from the currency of the country in which the property is located, e.g. a Yen mortgage for a property in Europe), as involving another currency may make your long-term planning both more risky and more complicated. See Chapter 26: Foreign Currencies.

In any case, be sure to shop around and ask your qualified financial adviser for information and advice as well. Make sure you know about all fees involved in the refinancing of your mortgage. Detailed comparisons will be necessary to ensure you get the best deal possible and are not surprised by fees, charges and other payments that were overlooked.

Many lenders, when confronted with a borrower wanting to change mortgage providers, will try to match the best offer you could obtain elsewhere; switching mortgage lenders might not become necessary. This would result in lower interest payments while remaining with the same lender (and without the fees and charges required to change mortgage providers).

Whenever there is a change in your mortgage or mortgage payments, be sure to update your budget accordingly.

100% Mortgage

In some cases, a mortgage for the entire 100% of the value of the property can be taken out. Not every mortgage provider offers this option. This form of mortgage is expensive as interest to be paid is typically higher than on non-100% mortgages and a certain fee might be applicable for a higher mortgage indemnity guarantee.

Islamic Mortgages

As mentioned earlier, Islamic mortgages have been developed to cater for the needs of this special market. They work in such a manner that either:

- the bank buys the property and, at the end of a specified term, sells it at a higher price agreed by both parties; the payments for this mortgage are made by the borrower paying instalments for rent and for gradually buying the mortgage lender's share of the property; or
- both bank and borrower buy the house, with the borrower holding a small stake only and paying rent to the bank who acts as a landlord until the entire amount is paid. Again, the payment for this is made with the borrower paying instalments for rent and for gradually buying the mortgage lender's share of the property.

An Islamic mortgage ensures that a Muslim homebuyer can afford to buy his or her dream home in any country while still complying fully with universal Islamic rules.

REVERSE MORTGAGES

A reverse mortgage allows a property owner (above a certain age) to use the property to receive payments instead of making payments. These payments can come in a lump sum, as monthly instalments or as a credit line. This means that, unlike a loan for which the borrowed amount continuously *decreases*, with a reverse mortgage the borrowed amount continuously *increases*. This growing loan debt is secured by the value of the property.

The sum received has to be repaid only when the owner moves out, sells the property or dies. Upon the death of the borrower the house is sold and any proceeds exceeding the amount owed under the reverse mortgage go to the estate. Alternatively, the heirs of the estate can opt to pay back the remaining loan without selling the property. If the property market goes up, as it has in the USA and UK over the past decade, the amount going to the estate might be substantial; likewise the amount to be paid back by the heirs might not be too big in relation to the value of the property.

One issue to watch out for is that the rate providers charge can be very high indeed. If these products are new to you, you should be especially careful to invest the time to understand the full costs of a reverse mortgage *before* signing up.

Professional advice may be particularly valuable here to untangle the web of rates and fees in this unfamiliar territory.

WHAT TO LOOK FOR

Before taking out a mortgage, ask yourself if you can really afford to buy the property. Remember to look at the total costs of owning a home, to take into consideration all payments, fees and extra costs involved in property ownership. Many people overlook property maintenance costs when calculating what they can afford. For example, utilities and property tax as well as contingencies for repairs (which are so often unexpected and untimely) need to be anticipated.

As financial adviser Arthur Lim points out, it is important not to stretch yourself to the absolute limit and not to deplete emergency funds when making decisions about property acquisition and mortgage debts.

When deciding upon the term of a mortgage, keep in mind that a longer mortgage term may mean lower monthly payments, but will also mean higher overall interest payments.

It may also be useful to provide for the unexpected when making your mortgage decision: What happens if you lose your job? What happens if interest rates rise? What happens if you fall seriously ill? All these factors and more must be taken into account when contemplating the 'right' mortgage.

When calculating how much mortgage you can afford, it may help use one of the many mortgage calculators freely available on the internet, or speak with a financial planner or banker to give you the expert advice you need. Property purchases, and their finance, can be some of the most important personal decisions individuals make throughout their lives!

❧ 12 ❧

TRANSPORTATION
AND VEHICLE PURCHASE

For many people, a car is the ultimate status symbol. From Ford to Ferrari, from Proton to Porsche, from Mazda to Mercedes, the spectrum of cars and their social value is a wide one.

Some global car markets are 'performance' markets, in which cars are purchased for their speed, handling or engineering. In Germany, for example, which is home to some of the best engineered products in the world, cars are purchased for performance rather than flashiness. Even the model numbers of high-end Mercedes sports cars are removed by discreet owners to obscure the expensive model name.

By comparison, the Asian car market is known as a 'statement' market, in which the status of the car — and often its astronomical price — may be more important to its owner than its handling capabilities. In such an environment, cars have a particularly high social value. Buyers often stretch to acquire the highest status model they can afford. In Singapore, for example, only a very lucky few can afford to pay for their dream car without having to borrow a significant amount of money. The vast majority of cars in Singapore are paid for by car loans as the overall costs for purchasing a car are very high when compared with European countries or the USA. The high price is due to import duties and other taxes levied on the price of the vehicle, as well as the certificate of entitlement (COE), which is a requirement for all vehicle owners.

Car Loans

Car loans make it possible to purchase a vehicle more easily, and perhaps earlier, than would be the case otherwise. In any case, the total amount borrowed and the term of the loan selected can create a significant outflow of monthly payments for many years. New vehicle buyers also need to budget for the additional costs they will incur when operating a car.

Perhaps the greatest cost of car ownership is hidden from many owners. Each year the value of a car declines as it ages and accumulates more mileage. For some, a car is known as a 'declining asset' since the value almost always drops over time.

While all of the operating costs and interest paid on a car loan should be included in your budget, the value of a vehicle should be reflected in the 'Other Assets' category on your Personal Wealth Schedule. This value will obviously decline over time as your vehicle ages.

OTHER TRANSPORT-RELATED COSTS

Insurance: In addition to car purchase or loan costs, you should also make sure you budget for car insurance and vehicle-associated taxes. It is obligatory for every registered car to have motor insurance.

Car insurance protects yourself and others in case of an accident. As mentioned in Chapter 10: Insurance, you may benefit from a good driving record as this, plus a claim-free insurance history, can bring down insurance payments by more than half.

Taxes: As mentioned in Chapter 8: Taxes, many countries have a road tax levied on registered vehicles. Road tax is payable either biannually or annually and is based, in most countries, on a vehicle's engine capacity. It also depends on the kind of engine, i.e. diesel or petrol.

Electronic Road Pricing (ERP), as well as serving as a deterrent for drivers to enter high-traffic areas, is another form of road tax, or toll. This cost should also be calculated in your transportation budget.

Parking: Annual parking costs, which can build up over time, especially if you drive to work, should be included in your transportation budget. Parking costs may be in the form of coupons, season parking, electronic or straight forward cash. All these expenses need to be taken into account.

Petrol: When budgeting for transportation, you will need to make an allowance for petrol. You may have to be ready to revisit this category periodically as petrol prices rise and fall with world oil prices.

Maintenance, repairs and inspections: Repairs and other car maintenance costs should also be taken into account when planning your transportation budget. These costs tend to occur on an irregular basis, so it is important to set aside a realistic allowance in order to avoid unpleasant surprises down the road. Bearing in mind that car ownership can involve a lot more than just vehicle purchase, you will need to be sure you include all of the relevant costs in order to build a sensible and accurate Wealth Wisdom Plan for your transportation needs.

Taxi and public transport: Taxi fares and public transport costs should also to be taken into account for occasional alternative transport costs.

෨ 13 ෨

CREDIT CARDS AND CONSUMER FINANCE

Sadly, far too many of us have too much credit card debt and pay too much interest on those debts.

The annual rate payable to borrow using a credit card is usually between 15% and 20% in most countries. This can add up to substantial amounts if spending by credit card is not controlled.

Credit cards can pose multiple traps: Spending is much harder to control than when using cash, fees are incurred without realising it, and excessive debt can result from less controlled spending. The hapless consumer can even end up paying interest on interest if payments are not made in time.

There are far better ways to manage our finances than to run up debts and pay these high interest rates. Your Wealth Wisdom Plan should help you to take a rational approach to your debts. This may well mean paying off your credit card bills every month and either borrowing money from cheaper sources or deferring your purchases until you have a greater cushion of cash and can make those purchases interest-free.

HIGH COST OF CREDIT CARD FINANCE

Credit card payments often include high interest charges for debts from past months which have not been paid off. Additional charges may be incurred for cash advance or foreign currency exchange services, as well as for spending over your credit limit. You may also be charged an annual fee for the use of your credit card. If agreed payments are not met in time, further penalties can also apply.

OTHER FORMS OF CONSUMER FINANCE

Many people take out loans to cover the cost of specific goods they wish to purchase, such as electronics or furniture. These loans have to be serviced and will reduce your spending power until the debt is paid off. Such loan obligations need to be taken into account in your Wealth Wisdom Plan and you should check for affordability of the purchase (can you really afford it in the context of your plan?) as well as the interest rate to be charged.

HOW MUCH DEBT CAN YOU AFFORD?

If discipline and diligence are not applied, using a credit card instead of cash and running up a series of consumer loans can lead to excessive spending and unhealthy spending habits, which only become apparent when the credit card bills come in.

Credit card companies try to encourage us to spend by offering reward points for the use of their cards and other similarly tempting promotions. Reward points, which can be traded in for goods or services, may seem attractive, but are only part of a financially healthy approach to financial management if the expenses incurred on such cards are under control.

All too fast, people can fall into a debt trap by overspending because they mistakenly believe they have sufficient funds available for their purchases. Very often this mistake is made because they did not have an overview of their finances, a costly miscalculation.

Failing to pay credit card and other loans will result in a less than perfect credit record which can, in turn, mean being denied credit later on or paying higher rates for future borrowings.

How Many Cards do You Have?

Many people have more than one credit card. Arguments for more than one card range from "I get more discount with card X at Shop Y", to "Some merchants do not accept this card so I need an alternative", to "My other card(s) can't be used now because I haven't paid my instalments".

This last example illustrates how it becomes easier for individuals without a plan or overall control to fall into the debt trap of borrowing to pay for borrowing; a vicious circle from which it is very difficult to escape.

If you do not know how to escape from this trap, you might wish to contact community advice services in your country who can help people with credit problems. They may be able to help show you how to break the circle. These advice services also provide debt checks and give you a better understanding of the full situation and realistic options available where you live.

OTHER TYPES OF CARDS

In addition to credit cards, providers offer a range of other cards:

Debit cards: Payments made by debit card still offer the convenience of not having to pay in cash when purchasing goods, but avoid opening up the debt trap as all payments are immediately deducted from your bank account.

Charge cards: As opposed to credit cards, charge cards require that purchases made throughout the billing period are paid off in full once the bill comes in.

Store cards: These cards allow customers to purchase goods in the issuing store, perhaps at a discount, and not have to pay for the goods immediately. While store cards may seem to be convenient, the downside is the extremely high interest rates charged for such purchases.

In the UK, for example, store cards charge interest of up to 30% per year. The UK Competition Commission now requires store card issuers charging interest rates of more than 25% to print a 'wealth warning' on monthly statements which reads: "The rate of interest charged on your account may be higher than on other sources of credit available to you. It may be costly for you to leave balances owing on your account after the interest free period".

Despite this warning, more than eleven million people in the UK have store cards amounting to a total outstanding debt of over £2 billion. Fifty seven percent of these borrowers fail to pay their bills in full at the end of the billing period. This may change as store card providers are now required to provide a direct debit option to enable card holders to pay off the amounts owed in full.

All credit and charge card providers offer different 'tiers' of cards, from basic to very high-end. These levels are reflected by correspondingly different fees, spending limits and services provided. If your income is above a certain threshold, certain levels of a card (for example, a Platinum) may require higher fees, but the associated benefits of such cards may outweigh the higher fees and charges. These benefits range from rewards to purchase protection, free supplementary cards, travel services 365 days a year, 24 hours a day, personalised concierge service and free travel insurance.

How Many Cards do You Need?

It has been demonstrated that a wallet full of cards may increase your actual spending.

Using different cards may also cause you to lose the overview of how much you have spent on which card, leading to unnecessary interest payments and other possible charges if payment deadlines are missed.

All of us appreciate the convenience of credit cards, replacing the need to carry cash. However, for many of us, the experience of handing over $50 in cash makes a much bigger impact on our shopping behaviour than does signing a credit card slip for the same amount. It may be a very healthy financial exercise to revert to the use of cash for some purchases to see just how fast and how easily our wallets empty, and where our funds actually go.

Total Costs of Credit Cards

Hardly anyone knows how much interest and fees he or she pays for outstanding loans, especially on credit cards.

To use but one example, if you use your credit card for a cash advance, interest is usually payable on this cash advance with immediate effect. It does not matter if you pay off the credit card bill at the end of the month or pay in instalments.

Interest on cash advances is still payable and, in many cases, charges are due as well.

CHECK YOUR STATEMENTS

As part of good housekeeping on the financial front, you should check your credit card statements as soon as they arrive. Check that charges are correct and, if you receive reward points, check that these have been calculated correctly.

These days, you should also check your statements carefully for the possibility of fraudulent use. Credit cards are all too often intercepted in the mail, stolen, fraudulently used on-line or 'copied' during transactions at a shop.

If you do not detect and object to such charges, you may have to pay for them yourself. You can also monitor your statement on-line, which will allow you to detect unauthorized transactions much faster and help avoid further inconvenience or financial damage by fraudsters.

∽ 14 ∾

EDUCATIONAL FINANCE

Derek Bok, former President of Harvard University, once said: "If you think education is expensive, try ignorance." Education is indeed expensive and will become even more so in the future, but ignorance can be a far more costly alternative.

In some European countries, practically all schooling is free, from primary school to university. In others, a university education is heavily subsidised. However, not everyone has access to low-cost or no-cost education. Some countries charge parents even for primary level education.

The need to finance your children's education may be one of the most important aspects of your personal financial planning, and most responsible parents budget for their children's education and start saving for that education as early as possible.

Private education can be extremely costly, even at secondary school level, as is the case for some international or boarding schools. But for most families, tertiary education, or even graduate school, usually constitutes the biggest expense. University education can amount to US$50,000 per year in extreme cases and it requires careful financial planning for most of us to afford such an expensive series of payments.

Apart from tuition fees, books and other study-related costs, travel costs, clothing, accommodation and the cost of living must also be calculated. These costs have been rising fast and can add up to considerable amounts every year, especially if you have several children. This is likely to be even more the case in the future, as the cost of education has been rising way above the rate of inflation.

A STRATEGIC APPROACH

The total amount of money required to fund your child's education can be substantial, but it can be saved for in a strategic manner over a long period of time. It is therefore important to start putting money aside when your child is very young.

It is never too early to start. As Chapter 16: Savings and Investments, explains, the earlier you start to save, the harder your capital and the interest accrued on it will work for you. This will result, in this instance, in more funds being available for education when you need them.

A university education may not be appropriate for all children, but other vocational training to prepare for a chosen career path can also be costly. As parents, we should try to set aside enough money to give our children the best possible start in life, whatever their capabilities.

What Types of Educational Funding are Available?

Endowment policies: These policies provide a low risk option to finance educational costs. Offered by insurance companies, they will pay out an agreed sum when your child reaches a specified age, for example 18-years-old, to cover educational expenses.

Endowment policies can include a clause which guarantees, in the event of the death or critical illness of the policy holder, no further premium payment will be necessary and the agreed sum will still be paid at the end of the term. The return on such policies is lower than on other investments but it comes with a correspondingly lower risk. Many parents do not want to take any risks at all when planning for their children's education.

Educational loans: If educational costs are too high and the family is unable to put other funding in place, educational loans can offer an alternative source of needed funds. These loans are usually taken out by the students themselves and are paid back once they finish university and earn a salary above a certain threshold.

Although this means the students start their working lives in debt, it also means they are equipped with a better education, hopefully enabling them to earn higher salaries. In turn, these higher salaries allow them to repay the loan more quickly.

In some countries, parents may take out loans at special rates to help them cope with education costs. In Singapore, for example, it is possible to use some CPF funds to pay for your children's tertiary education, providing that education is within Singapore. Repayment of this loan starts one year after the child's graduation and can extend for up to 12 years beyond that date.

Scholarships and grants: Scholarships and grants provide another way to fund education. A number of organisations award annual scholarships to enable capable students to obtain an education without any financial impediment.

Competition for such scholarships is high, but they are worth applying for as they might open new doors and learning opportunities for your child, with little or no application charge.

In some cases, scholarships come with a bond or other commitment to work for the organisation granting the scholarship for a certain period of time after graduation. Sponsoring organisations pick the very brightest talents and hope to have a return on their 'investment' by adding the chosen student's knowledge and skills to the knowledge pool of the organisation for a defined minimum term after graduation.

Some well-endowed private universities and some state-funded schools are able to give out financial aid based on the financial needs of an applicant. Information on student aid funds available can be obtained from the relevant school or university.

LET YOUR CHILD CONTRIBUTE

In the same way that responsible parents should plan and budget for their child's education, a responsible child should also contribute where he or she can.

Children can contribute directly towards their educational expenses by working part-time while at university or working full-time during holiday periods.

Not only will this help financially, it can also provide several other related benefits: your child can gain valuable work experience, achieve a new degree of personal and financial independence, learn a responsible attitude towards money, build self-esteem and know that they have been able to contribute to the family budget in an important way.

It can be a valuable learning experience for your child to take a part-time or holiday job at McDonald's, Starbucks or any other business. Such an experience will clearly show them that work is necessary to achieve what we want and need in life.

❧ 15 ❧

CHARITY AND PHILANTHROPY

Charity and philanthropy are an important part of our lives and therefore an important part of our personal financial plans. While not providing income or contributing to the accumulation of our material wealth, generosity to help those less fortunate than ourselves can be seen as a major element of our personal and spiritual development.

Charity and philanthropy — which can be defined as charity on a grander scale — allow us to contribute to the improvement of the quality of life in the world, or to the societies and the communities in which we live.

The spirit of charitable giving stretches far back in history as one of the oldest and most positive characteristics of human civilisation. Evidence has been found of gifts from the wealthy to the poor in Egyptian tombs over 4,000 years old.

The *Li Ki*, the Chinese 'Book of Rites' also echoed the same sentiments of generosity 3,000 years ago.

To whom can we give?

There is no shortage of opportunity in the world to help those who are less well-off than we are. Charitable donations can provide aid during crises such as earthquakes and the 2004 tsunami, or to help victims of SARS. Charitable contribution can also address longer-term problems such as health care or environmental issues.

Religious institutions are also major recipients of charitable donations, and have been so for thousands of years. At the end of the 18th century, charitable giving fell under four major headings, with most giving focused on local causes: the relief of poverty, the advancement of education, the advancement of religion and 'other purposes beneficial to the community'.

More recently, the range of causes to which one can donate has become far broader and includes advancement of the arts, assistance to the disabled and elderly, healthcare, animal protection, the environment and global human rights campaigns.

The selection of recipients for our material generosity is a very individual choice. Some donors choose local charities where there is a personal connection and a more immediate sense of contribution. Others prefer to give to spiritual institutions which have made a positive contribution to their own lives.

Yet others make an assessment which leads them to contribute to causes which are more remote from their daily lives. Some donors select the destination of their contributions based upon a more objective view of human need and the potential impact of their contribution.

How much should we give?

As with the destination of your charitable contribution, the amount contributed is also enormously personal; there is no universal guideline.

Almost every religion encourages or requires acts of generosity and material giving. Certain religious doctrines do give some guidance: The Christian religion cites charity, along with faith and hope, as supreme virtues. The Church of England encourages its members to give 5% of their income to charitable causes. Other UK institutions encourage a donation equivalent to at least 1% of income.

Islam has *zakat* as one of the five pillars of Islam, a word which carries with it a sense of both purification and growth: 2.5% of savings and valuables is seen as an appropriate level of charitable donation.

The Jewish tradition of *tzedakah* recommends a 10–20% donation of after-tax income, depending on the wealth of the individual.

To date, only the USA and Israel give more than 1% of their GDP to charity. The USA is particularly generous, partly due to the fact that charitable contributions are usually deductible from taxable income, unlike in other countries. Whether tax-inspired or not, nearly 90% of American households make some contribution to charity.

Internationally, the amount recommended for charitable giving ranges from 1–20% of annual income, with actual national averages slightly below the 1% threshold in most instances. In Singapore, the rate of personal giving is on average 0.5% of income.

How can we Give?

There are many ways to give financially to charity. Direct contribution is the easiest and most straightforward approach but other possibilities, such as life insurance policies with a named charity as the beneficiary, allow you to spread payments evenly over a lifetime to provide a large lump sum contribution in the future.

Money is not the Only Way to Give

Wealth Wisdom is about financial planning and hence focuses on the financial aspects of charity. There are, however, many other laudable ways to support charities and to help the needy.

Volunteering at a church or charitable institution can make a big difference, as can fund-raising. When funds are limited, it is worth thinking about these other ways in which you could contribute.

❧ 16 ❧

SAVINGS AND INVESTMENT

Asians are big savers. According to the AC Nielsen Global Consumer Confidence Survey of February 2006, more than half of what is left over after covering essential living expenses, goes into savings. Actual rates range from around 50% in Japan and Indonesia, to around 55% in Malaysia, Thailand, India, Hong Kong and Korea, to around 60% in Singapore and the Philippines. Taiwan tops the list with 62% of spare cash put into savings.

The USA, according to the Washington Times (31 January 2006) set a record low in 2005 of minus 0.5% — a 'negative savings rate'. A 'negative savings rate' means that an individual is spending more than 100% of his or her income, perhaps funded by credit card debt, banking loan lines, drawing down on savings or borrowing against the increased value of a house or shares.

What is the Difference between Savings and Investment?

The difference between savings and investment is that there is no risk of losing the initial capital in savings, which is possible in an investment. Investments tend to be riskier and hence have the potential (but by no means the certainty) of higher returns. For every dollar of savings, you will receive interest in addition to preserving your original capital. For investments, however, the original capital can increase (usually more than it would if the capital were put into savings as the higher risk usually pays a higher return) as well as decrease.

Cash Under the Mattress

Some people still keep significant amounts of cash at home as a kind of insurance. This is, to be honest, a very expensive and ineffective way of managing your capital. Not only are theft and fire grave risks, but you also pay heavily for the missed opportunity to earn risk-free interest on the capital.

Whether you put money into savings or investment depends on your personal profile: How much risk do you want to take? What do you want to achieve? Do you want your capital to grow but are not sure of the time frame? Do you want to take some risk and see if you can get higher returns in a shorter period of time?

What are your Savings Alternatives?

Within the savings category, there are a number of accounts into which you can place your savings.

Checking (current) accounts: Many checking accounts, especially those with a low balance, may yield the same rate of interest as cash under the mattress. Some banks may even charge you for the privilege of holding your money, or bill you for each cheque written. The only way to manage a checking account efficiently is to understand the full fees involved and avoid leaving excess funds in accounts which make the bank richer and you poorer than you need to be.

Savings accounts: Saving accounts pay more interest and are a popular savings tool. Depending on the jurisdiction, deposits in savings accounts may be insured against loss by the state. Interest is paid to the account holder, but the account holder may also have to pay bank fees if the amount in the account falls below a pre-set threshold.

It is wise to shop around (terms and conditions do vary) to ensure you get the maximum benefit out of your savings.

Chapter 20: Cash and Deposits, also provides more information about these products.

LONGER TERM SAVINGS

As with most things in the world of finance, less liquidity, or a more limited ability to access your funds on demand, yields a higher return on your money. Although your return may be higher, you need to be sure that you do not need access to your money within the period for which your money is tied up. There can be substantial charges involved for early withdrawal. These charges can bring the total rate of return to below that of short-term deposits.

Again, it is important to shop around to get the best rates before selecting a long-term savings account.

START TO SAVE EARLY

If you do not withdraw anything from your saved or invested funds and instead use the interest earned to reinvest in the same product over a very long period at an attractive rate, the end result can be very impressive indeed. Over the years, the accumulated amount can turn into a handsome sum, particularly if you start to save early. The effect of interest building up on a growing base of initial investment, plus past interest, is called 'compound interest'. Over a long period of time, compound interest can have a powerful impact on the value of your savings and investment and one of the key insights from a Wealth Wisdom Plan is the power of early saving. A simple example illustrates the point.

If an individual sets aside $25,000 at age 25 and invests this amount in a portfolio yielding a 10% return per year (reinvesting all proceeds but not adding any new funds), this sum would have grown into more than $1.1 million at age 65.

If you have a time horizon of 25 years, compound interest turns this initial $25,000 into more than $270,000, an increase of more than ten times the amount invested. These numbers would be lower if a capital gains tax were levied on the interest income generated.

It is easy to calculate what you need to save to generate what you want to have at a future date.

If you want to have $500,000 in 10 years and your expected rate of return is 5%, you would need to set aside slightly more than $306,000 in a lump sum now or pay slightly more than $37,800 each year over 10 years to achieve the same result. If your expected rate of return is 8%, you would need to set aside slightly more than $231,000 to reach the same goal, or slightly less than $32,000 annually over 10 years.

From these numbers, which do not show such spectacular gains over a shorter period of time, we can again see the power of compound interest and the value of early saving.

You can calculate compound interest on various websites available online, or speak to a financial advisor who can help you to make the calculations and understand their implications from your perspective.

WHY DO YOU WANT TO INVEST?

It is imperative for you to know *why* you want to invest:

Is this an investment to top-up your income in the short-term? An investment to build up capital to spend in retirement? An investment for your children's educational costs? Another type of investment? The answer to *why* you want to invest will play a large role in determining *what* you should invest in.

You can invest in many different asset categories ranging from property (both residential and non-residential), to your own business (or a stake in a shared business), shares, bonds, mutual funds, pensions, gold and commodities, arts and antiques, private equity (representing ownership in businesses whose shares are not quoted on a listed exchange), derivatives, and others.

Asset allocation — the disciplined approach of saving and investing your money in a careful balance across more than one category of savings or investment products — is an important exercise to be undertaken *before* making decisions about how you invest. Chapter 18 gives more information on asset allocation.

❦ 17 ❧

MAKING IT WORK FOR YOU

Armed with the information and guidance detailed in the preceding chapters, you are now ready to enter your own information in the Annual Budget and Monthly Budget Tracker at the back of this book. With this practical step, you will be well on your way to completing your own Wealth Wisdom Plan.

You can complete your plan manually, using the paper forms included here or you may wish to use the on-line versions available on the Channel NewsAsia website.

If you are using the paper forms, you may find it useful to make a few photocopies of each page before you begin. This will allow you to make corrections without spoiling your only copy and also be ready for future planning exercises at no cost.

The following steps will describe how to go about completing forms I and II for your own Wealth Wisdom Plan.

COMPLETING THE ANNUAL BUDGET

1. Collect and prepare the documents and files for the current year as described in Chapter 4: Your Wealth Wisdom Plan.

   You may find it useful to do an historic budget for the last financial year to ensure you haven't forgotten anything, but this is optional, as it is more important to improve the future than to review the past.

   Do not try to rush. You may want to pause to reconsider how much to spend on insurance or how to reduce transport or other costs as you go along. It will be the quality of the final output, not the speed with which you fill out the Annual Budget, which will determine the value of the exercise.

   Do not just accept existing income and cost levels as set in stone. One of the great advantages of doing a full plan will be found in the improvements you make as you go along. The more challenging and active the process, the better.

2. Multiply by 12 the monthly income or expenditure figure in column A and enter this amount in column B to obtain the annual total of your regular monthly expenditures.

3. Enter any annual or other income or expenses which are *not* regular monthly amounts as 'irregular' items in column C.

   This may include one-off annual insurance premiums, road tax, charitable donations, gifts, etc.

4. Add columns B and C together to get total annual income and expenditure figures for all listed items and enter these figures in column D.

5. Calculate the total amount available for savings and investment at the bottom of the form by subtracting total expenses from net income.

6. As a final check, review all the numbers from an overall perspective. Do they look right? Have you forgotten anything?

Your review should rely on your judgment as much as your number skills.

USING THE ON-LINE FORMS

If you are using the on-line version of the forms, there are only a few differences in the process. The on-line version of the templates can be used just as the paper forms with a few additional instructions as follows:

1. Download the templates from the website.
2. Remember to save updated versions of the file as you go along.
3. The on-line Annual Budget form will automatically multiply the figure in your first column by 12 and insert the total in column B.
4. The Annual Budget form will add columns B and C for you and automatically enter the total in column D.
5. Finally, the on-line Annual Budget form will automatically calculate and enter your funds available for savings and investment.

COMPLETING THE MONTHLY BUDGET TRACKER

The Monthly Budget Tracker can be used throughout the year to track actual income and expenses against your budget.

Using either the paper or on-line version of the Monthly Budget Tracker, enter the expected monthly income and expense figures for each item calculated in the Annual

Budget. This figure should include both the regular monthly items and the irregular payments you need to make. If your vehicle insurance is due in May, then your May insurance payment will reflect this. This will give you a benchmark for each category for each month, against which you can measure your financial progress.

Recording your actual income and expenses on a monthly basis not only helps to keep you on track for the current year, it will also make it easier for you to document your income and expenses in the future and give you a realistic base upon which to build your Wealth Wisdom Plan.

Although the most complete approach would involve entering an amount each month in each column, you may want to take a simpler approach and place an X in a box only if you overspend. The boxes can be left blank if you are within budget. This simplified approach can highlight where you need to focus your efforts to get back on track.

BETTER RESULTS ARE THE REAL OBJECTIVE

The ultimate objective of these planning and tracking exercises is to enable you to gain full control over your finances and to realise the full potential of your wealth creation capability.

By completing these two forms, and putting as much thought as possible into their content, you will be on top of all aspects of your own income and expenses.

By following the content of your plan, you will demonstrate a higher level of discipline and a more professional approach to the management of your affairs. That attitude and approach should soon lead you to the realisation of better results from your efforts to grow your own wealth.

Part III

SAVINGS AND INVESTMENTS

❧ 18 ❧

OVERVIEW AND ASSET ALLOCATION

Asset allocation — the allocation of your capital to different asset classes such as stocks, bonds, property, derivatives, private equity, gold and commodities — is the foundation upon which you can best build your own fortune.

An enormous amount of analysis by the world's best investment professionals shows that the real key to wealth creation is asset allocation and a disciplined, long-term approach to savings and investment.

What does not work for almost everyone is stock picking, trying to time the market, investing on rumours, flipping in and out of individual stocks, taking excessive exposure to one stock without thorough analysis, or even over-investing in one category of assets.

There are two conceptual elements, *portfolio theory* and *scientific asset allocation*, which provide the foundation for modern asset allocation.

Portfolio theory: The first element of understanding is that a collection of different asset classes, also called a 'portfolio' of assets, set up carefully and rebalanced over time, will perform better than any individual asset class. In fact, analysis over an extended time frame now shows that 90% of the value created or lost in an investment portfolio is driven by the asset classes you select rather than by the individual investments selected within the portfolio.

The stock market can go up or down quite dramatically at different times, with many shares tending to follow, at least to some extent, overall market movements. The property market, shares and bonds all tend to go down when interest rates go up, commodities and some 'short' funds (funds that pick investments that make money when the markets go down) may do the opposite. Private equity funds raised at stock market peaks do less well than those raised in market lows.

A blend of asset classes can weather inevitable storms of change better and protect the creation of long-term value in your own portfolio.

Scientific asset allocation: Once an investor has decided to invest across more than one asset class, the question arises as to how best to allocate capital between so many 'classes' of investment.

Unfortunately, there is no one 'right' answer to this question. Your own asset allocation will depend upon your personal savings and investment objectives, your appetite for risk (without which there is no reward in a financial market) and the capabilities of you and your adviser to provide information and select attractive investments within each asset class elected.

How then can an individual best approach the issue of asset allocation?

SET YOUR OBJECTIVES

Every investor's portfolio objectives will vary. Some may want to protect capital for retirement. Some may want to generate income from which to pay living expenses. Others may want to get rich quickly and be willing to consider a blend of investments which are high risk/high return. This last objective would probably not be of interest to, for example, a more conservative younger investor or an older couple with a more conservative set of portfolio goals. For more details on how to set your wealth objectives, please refer to Chapter 3.

UNDERSTAND THE ASSET CLASSES YOU SELECT

It is also important to be careful and honest about estimating your own ability to understand fully the nature and likely performance of the assets you purchase. It is absolutely essential that you *do not select any asset class or specific investment you do not fully understand.*

There are many standard asset classes more easily understood by the small or new investor: publicly quoted shares, bonds, property, deposits, emerging market equities, gold, commodities and other asset classes can, with little extra effort, be understood at a high level by most investors. These asset classes are discussed in more detail later in this book.

Far too may investors have been disappointed by their inability to predict the negative results they suffer from a complex instrument, such as a derivative or highly geared property investment, which they did not fully understand when they made their investment. More than one investor has seen his entire savings wiped out by inappropriately risky investment choices.

Choose According to Your Appetite for Risk

There is a hierarchy of risk between asset classes. Junk bonds, some spectacular hedge funds, private equity transactions and highly levered property deals can lead to a high return or to a total loss of capital invested. The same is true for direct business investments.

At the other end of the scale, there are risk-free instruments in the form of government bonds, and near risk-free assets such as federally guaranteed deposits in healthy banks. The return on these lower risk assets will, of course, be far lower than the potential return on more speculative investments.

The balance of asset classes within a portfolio and between these risk categories will depend upon the portfolio objectives and the overall financial situation of each investor.

Overconfidence

Almost all humans are overly confident about their abilities. Ninety percent of drivers, for example, think that they are better drivers than average, which obviously cannot be the case. Overconfidence can be a very expensive conceit in the financial world. INSEAD professor Anil Gaba has provided evidence that people overestimate their ability to select a good investment *and* hold on to bad investments for too long. As you set out on your selection of asset classes and define your approach to buying and selling within each, it may well be worth remembering the true limits of one's ability. Again, consult your financial adviser to determine what asset allocation is best in your situation.

Take a Holistic View

It is important to understand each individual asset class selection and the investments within it. It is equally, if not more, important to understand how the entire portfolio will behave in different economic environments. You will need to understand how a particular portfolio will behave if interest rates or stock markets go up and down. The answers may not be obvious.

One investment guru in the USA described a portfolio like a cake, where individual ingredients, such as butter, sugar, flour and eggs behave very differently when combined together. He also noted that each 'cake' had very different characteristics at different temperatures. One portfolio could do far better than another when specific markets were either hot or cold.

Re-Balance Periodically

The only constant in the financial world is change.

Your objectives will change with different life stages and with the development of your wealth profile. You may change your liquidity preferences. You may change your risk/reward approach. You may have an increase in the funds available and hence have sufficient funds to access more limited asset classes like bigger property deals, private equity or hedge funds. You could still shift from an income objective to a capital growth objective.

The relevant market could also change quite substantially. Interest rates, currencies, tax policies, stock markets, property markets and all other exchanges will evolve over time.

Asset allocations should be reviewed at least once a year on an overall basis. Some individuals review and refine their investment choices on a quarterly basis, or even more frequently. Changes should also be made as and when necessary to re-balance your assets to reflect the most current views on individual investment objectives and external market developments.

GATHER INFORMATION AND VIEWS

We live in an age where enormous amounts of information and many different views are available on asset allocation models and individual investments. It is essential to stay informed about the options available to you and also about the services advisers can provide to meet your needs.

While information from financial advisers may be easy to obtain and important to help you make decisions, the beneficiaries of your investments — you and your family — will hold the responsibility for the asset allocation model selected and its ultimate results.

USE THE BEST INDEPENDENT PROFESSIONALS

A good and honest adviser can be essential in determining the best asset allocation model and selecting reliable investments within it. Make sure you have a thorough discussion with your advisers and be confident that your needs and objectives are being fully considered.

One key principle when selecting an adviser is to be very careful about not selecting one who has a vested interest in the products he is selling to you.

Many investors have found that their investments were not made in best-of-class products which maximised their wealth, but were focussed only on those products which gave their advisers a large commission on each order and the biggest bonus at the end of the year.

WATCH THE FEES

Many managers who purport to select stocks well are often out-performed by an index fund which is merely the average of all stocks in an exchange and relatively cheap to buy, in terms of both fees and commissions.

While the value of a portfolio approach is very clear, there is a hidden risk on the cost side. It is easy to stack up fees on individual investments, fees on mutual fund operation, fees to professional advisers, etc. Good advisers might be 'worth their weight in gold', but shouldn't charge the equivalent amount to their customers.

For long-term wealth creation, it is essential to have an asset allocation model that provides you with the performance you want, *after* all fees and charges are taken into account.

⧼ 19 ⧽

PROPERTY

Many great Asian fortunes have been built on a foundation of investment in property; many more individuals have created a substantial amount of personal wealth by buying their own home and holding onto it through the years.

As Mark Twain said over one hundred years ago, "Land is a great investment because they aren't making any more of it." The scarcity of land, general economic growth, increasing wealth of individuals and easy availability of home mortgages make the property market one in which all investors need to consider participating.

From a planning perspective, purchase and ownership of a primary residence, especially with a mortgage, has a big influence on your expenses (mortgage, insurance, upkeep, renovation and others) taxes (in most countries) and your asset allocation model.

If you own other property, it may have an impact on income as well.

OWNING YOUR OWN HOME

Owning your own home has been the best single source of wealth creation in many countries for many years. Property ownership also provides a rent-free home upon retirement, assuming the mortgage has been paid off in prior years. In addition, in some countries, a house or flat which has appreciated in value may be used as security to borrow money, reducing the cost of borrowing and providing tax benefits.

In addition to the financial benefits that can come from home ownership, there is also a psychological benefit in the peace of mind that ownership creates.

While most people's main property investment is their primary residence, there are many other property investment opportunities available. You may wish to purchase additional properties for rent or sale, purchase shares in listed property companies or invest in funds which make investments in properties. You can also invest indirectly in the property market by buying shares in construction companies or other businesses related to the development of the property market.

Some companies with more than one line of business have property divisions as well as, for example, consumer products businesses. Investing in these shares gives you the opportunity to invest in property and achieve some diversification in your investment, spreading your risk across more than one sector.

Property investments, made directly or through shares, can be held in a wide variety of property categories with different risk and return potential by market. Commercial, office, retail, residential, government housing, hotel, shopping centre, undeveloped land, capital city, secondary cities, suburbs, country, agricultural, freehold and leasehold all have different financial characteristics. Obviously, these categories vary enormously from country to country and over time.

Property is a global game. You can invest in shares or properties in the USA, UK, Europe, Asia or in emerging markets. Needless to say, if you are investing in a property or property shares in a foreign country, you need to be aware of the currency implications of the investment as described in Chapter 26: Foreign Currencies.

Real estate investment trusts, or REITs, are another form of property investment available globally as will be described below. These trusts, known as REITs, are publicly traded securities backed by property assets. REITs pay a return to investors based on the yield of the properties in the REIT portfolio.

UPS AND DOWNS

As everyone in Asia knows, the property market can move up or down with great variations over the years. A boom in the period up to 1997 was followed by a big drop in many countries during the Asian Economic Crisis. In the USA, a long period of housing price increases has contributed enormously to the wealth (on paper at least) of the 70% of Americans who own their own homes.

When the property market takes a big drop in value, some people may find themselves in the position of owning a home whose value in the market is less than the value of the mortgage. This unfortunate situation is called 'negative equity' and could have been seen in many homes in, for example, Hong Kong in the late 1990s.

HERD MENTALITY

While herd mentality may contribute to the rise in property prices by focusing the investments of many people in the same area, it can also be dangerous in other circumstances.

One investment expert, for example, predicts that in Singapore too many owners of five-room homes are planning on downsizing to three-room homes as their families leave. These owners are counting on using the difference in price between five- and three-bedroom units to fund their retirement.

His view is that the big increase in the number of five-room homes coming onto the market at the same time will drive down prices for that size unit, while, at the same time, an increase in demand for three-room units will drive those prices up. He sees the spread in price narrowing, which may cause forward-thinking Singaporeans to rethink their longer-term financial strategies if this is indeed the case.

RESIDENTIAL PROPERTY

Buying a home needs to be considered on two important dimensions. On the one hand, it is a major lifestyle choice involving proximity to schools, family, financial burdens, transportation and other personal aspects of life.

On the other hand, buying a home is one of the biggest — and maybe *the* biggest — financial investment decision you will make. While the personal and lifestyle decisions are very important, the purchase of your primary residence should also be seen as a cornerstone of your wealth plans.

As such, a number of questions need to be answered in an analytical manner as well as dealing with the emotional considerations involved. Any potential buyer will need to have answers to such questions as:

- How long are we likely to be living here?
- Is the neighbourhood likely to increase or decrease in value? Is it likely to be disturbed by major building projects which may limit enjoyment of a property (but may add value in the longer term)?

- Can the house be upgraded? Expanded? What will this cost? With what benefit on sale?
- Can I afford it?
- What are the alternatives?
- What are the full costs of ownership?
- What are the full risks and opportunities of ownership?
- Is it better to rent or buy now? What is better in the long term?
- What is my target return on the investment?
- How can I maximise my return?
- What timing is best for my strategy?

What You should do before You Buy

Once you have decided you would like to become a property owner, and before committing to a purchase, it is important to shift your mindset from the thrill of finding a home in which you wish to live to the tough-minded assessment of the choice in terms of a financial investment. You will need to ensure that the property, neighbourhood and financial terms of purchase, insurance and mortgage are all entirely acceptable to you.

In this frame of mind, it is important to have thorough surveys done to establish the structural condition of the property. Even in well-established areas of London, for example, where houses have stood for over 100 years, there can be land subsidence and major foundation work required to fix resulting problems. At a smaller scale, prolonged exposure to damp, dry rot or other costly problems should be exposed and reflected in the price.

You should also be aware of any development plans in the area which might affect the structural integrity or commercial value of the property. Is there an underground line being built nearby? Is there a major road alteration coming up? Are new schools or new shopping centres being built?

In all cases, the financing options need to be understood before you begin your search. The amount you can afford to borrow, will probably affect the price range and location of the property you are seeking. It is important to speak to more than one banker — and to complete your Wealth Wisdom Plan — before setting out on a search for your dream home.

CREATING INCOME FROM PROPERTY

As well as the investment value you have created through property purchase, you may also be able to boost your income by renting all or part of the property. The amount you can earn from property rental will depend on several factors, including location, whether it is your primary or secondary residence (i.e. are you renting out one room or the whole property?), condition of the property, whether it is furnished or unfurnished and, of course, the current state of the rental market.

If you are a property owner above a certain age and about to retire, you may want to enjoy some income without having to rent out or sell your property during your lifetime. Although the rates offered may not be attractive when compared to other alternatives, a reverse mortgage could be considered. For more details, see Chapter 11: Mortgages, and Chapter 36: Retirement Planning.

NON-RESIDENTIAL PROPERTY

Investments in non-residential property such as an office building, land for development and other properties can be very attractive if done in an expert manner. Such non-residential property markets have performed very differently around the world over the past ten years, with some areas like the USA, UK and some emerging markets expanding rapidly. Others — parts of Asia that had benefited from decades of expansion decades for example — were declining or at least failing to provide interesting returns on investment when compared to other alternatives.

In all of these markets, there are countless opportunities for investment that require thorough investigation, careful planning and expert advice. Perhaps even more than usual, acquiring property will require the advice of more than one professional adviser.

Brokers, lawyers, surveyors, decorators, engineers and other experts can provide essential advice to ensure that your biggest investment is one which is most likely to perform as well as it possibly can.

FINANCIAL ASPECTS OF PROPERTY

There are many unique elements to investment in property: It is easier to borrow against property than it is against some other investments, tax treatments can create specific advantages for property investors, accounting treatment needs to be understood and any available subsidies or grants need to be applied for. Partnerships can be a valuable approach to development, as can the creation of a company or other entity to serve as a special purpose vehicle (known as an "SPV") which is set up solely for the purpose of buying, developing and selling a property.

It may be useful to understand the full range of options for financing non-residential property, and in particular to note potential changes in available funding.

Real Estate Investment Trusts (REITs)

Unlike bonds or money market certificates, which are usually issued against the general asset base of a government or corporation, a REIT is an investment backed by an identified set of properties. As the yield on the property rises and falls and as the value of the underlying property rises and falls, the value of the REIT changes over time.

The REIT's regular payment makes it an attractive alternative to a bond for some investors, though it is considered as part of a different asset class.

Created in the 1970s to allow small investors to participate in the property market, REITs have gone in and out of fashion over the years, rising in popularity when the property market is relatively strong.

Property Portfolio Principles

Once you have enough wealth to provide for your own home and to venture forth into the broader property market, there are some tips that may be useful in structuring your approach. Owning a collection of property assets has an additional set of principles that need to be considered in addition to all the basic elements of any single investment, such as taking professional advice, understanding risk, not getting over-stretched, etc. In developing a wider portfolio of properties, you should address a series of related issues:

Strategy: The first issue is to decide what you are looking to accomplish. Are you seeking to develop a flow of income or capital gain? Is your goal to create wealth for yourself or for your children or others?

Content: Second, what would you like your portfolio to look like? Should it be diversified or concentrated, high or low risk, short- or long-term? The individual properties and the collection of all properties will need to be thought through carefully to meet your overall objectives.

Ownership structure: One of the biggest mistakes property investors make, is to bundle their individual properties together, so that failure in one investment can bring down the whole portfolio. Keep each investment separate if at all possible. Keep your family home away from the risks of external investments. Avoid cross-collateralisation, which means staying away from using one building as security for one or more other properties.

Many wealthy property investors have lost their entire fortune by ignoring these rules and taking excessive risk with their financial and ownership structures. We can learn from their expensive mistakes and plan to develop our investments in a way which avoids the pitfalls into which they tumbled.

Benefits of scale: As your property portfolio grows, you may find opportunities for benefits from your increased size. Insurance may be cheaper. Builders may offer bigger discounts for longer-term projects or a series of projects.

Market timing: Unlike the experts' recommendation not to try to time the market for investments in, for example, the stock market, timing is essential in any property market. The USA had a very difficult time in 1989 and 1990, parts of Asia did the same in 1997 and 1998 and Japan had a long decline from 1989 for more than a decade. China, the UK and other markets have had similar ups and downs. Timing, and the knowledge of when to buy and sell, is a critical element in any property strategy.

Risk management: As you get more experienced in your property investments, there will be opportunities to manage your risk which may be worth considering. You may want to bring in a partner or partners on a deal. You may want to invest in more than one property, in more than one sector or in more than one country. You may want to 'hedge' your investment through a capital market product that protects the value of your investment.

Expertise: You may also want to focus on developing expertise in a particular area of property investing. Distressed commercial property, high-end hotels, suburban malls and other areas can benefit from the development of specific knowledge and applicable expertise.

Asian flavour: The rise of Asia's economic power and increasing impact on economies far from home has opened up opportunities to transplant some home-grown knowledge into the more developed property markets of the world. In the USA, for example, some specialist developers in California are building homes specially designed for multi-generational Asian families.

The homes, which combine a small flat for the grandparents with a larger home for the children and grandchildren, can be mortgaged as a single unit and jointly owned. This creates both financial and tax benefits across the generations, while providing a home well suited for the lifestyles of all three generations.

In London, at the high end of the market, an entrepreneur is developing large luxury flats with two parking spaces in an unusually large basement parking lot and staff flats for housekeepers in a highly secure building, thus accommodating the lifestyles of some of Asia's wealthiest families.

Contingency planning: It is a truism that renovation of a primary residence almost always takes twice as long and costs twice as much as originally envisioned. This can wreak havoc on your plans. You may be financially stretched far more than you want, may suffer disruptions to your personal life and may have more than one heated discussion with a broker, architect, builder or spouse.

Budgeting for contingencies may get you through this experience with better memories and a plan more intact than might otherwise be the case.

KEY DECISION

As we said at the beginning of this chapter, and even as illustrated on the cover of this book, successful property ownership can be the key to increased wealth, a happy family home and peace of mind. On the other hand, failed investments in property have had just the opposite effect.

Since decisions with regard to property are so significant, you will want to be extra sure that you have considered all of the angles, taken all of the advice you need and planned for whatever contingencies may arise.

≈ 20 ≈

CASH AND DEPOSITS

Under-managing our cash and bank deposits is a very common mistake.

Through inertia, laziness or simply by being too busy with the other elements of our lives, we may not pay enough attention to our cash and deposits. We may not shop around for the best deals or we may leave our cash in low yielding checking or savings accounts for far too long. We may let our savings or checking accounts slip below the required minimum balance and so receive less interest than we should. We may not track our checking account balances and incur bank charges for returned, or 'bounced', cheques due to insufficient funds.

Another classic error is to make the false economy of not paying off our credit card debts each month even though we have the means to do so in our savings or checking accounts. Although we may be receiving 2-3% interest on our savings, we may be paying more than 20% in interest and charges on the outstanding credit card balance. The net result: we lose and the credit card company wins.

A carefully controlled cash management programme can help us to maximise the interest from our savings and minimise the interest and fees paid in other accounts.

'You Gotta Shop Around'

This line from a well-known song captures a key message. Don't just give all your new business to your old bank out of habit. Different banks have different products available at different rates. Some will be better suited to your needs, and more profitable for you, than others.

As part of your Wealth Wisdom Plan, you may want to visit at least three banks and compare their products and services. But before you start to shop around, it is useful to have a clear idea of the types of deposit products on offer.

Types of Deposit and Cash Management Accounts

Broadly, there are six types of deposit and cash management accounts. As with most financial products, the longer you leave your money in an interest-paying account, the more interest you will receive. The range of accounts, from lowest yielding to highest, is as follows:

Regular checking (current) accounts: These accounts allow you to effect transactions without using cash. A regular checking account pays no interest and has no withdrawal limits. You will probably be charged for returned cheques, extra copies of statements, overdrafts and other services which can be avoided through careful management. More and more, banks are also charging for each cheque written. It may be better to set up a series of direct debits to avoid these charges if your account operates on a fee-per-cheque basis.

Interest-bearing checking accounts: These accounts allow you to write cheques but do pay some interest on the balance in your account. They usually make charges similar to those on a checking account for 'bounced' cheques, overdrafts and other services. There may be a minimum monthly balance requirement.

Money market accounts: These accounts pay more interest than standard savings and checking accounts but usually limit the number of cheques that you can write. There may also be a limit on the number of withdrawal transactions per month. By limiting these transactions, the bank can reduce its account operating costs and pass some of the savings on to you.

Saving accounts: Basic savings accounts pay interest and do not allow cheques as a means to withdraw or transfer funds. These days, most cash withdrawals are made from ATMs, which provide easy access at no charge (though you may be charged if you withdraw money from another bank's ATM machine). Some banks offer free checking accounts if you also have a savings account with them.

Savings clubs: Some banks offer regular savings club schemes whereby you pay in a set amount every week. This approach may be used for a particular purpose, for example a Christmas or holiday fund, or may be more general in nature. While savings clubs can be a convenient and easy way to build some savings discipline, you should ensure that it is paying the best interest rate available to you before making a major commitment.

Certificates of deposit: Also called 'CDs', these accounts pay a higher interest than those mentioned above but require you to deposit your money for longer. The deposit term can range from one month to five years.

Certificates of deposit require a relatively high balance and may carry stiff penalties for early withdrawal. Many of them pay interest at a fixed rate, whether market interest rates go up or down.

MINIMUM BALANCES AND ANNUAL FEES

In order for you to avoid account management fees, many accounts require that a minimum balance be kept. This balance provides the bank with a floor level of profitability on your account.

To maximise returns on cash, every investor should make sure he or she is aware of, understands and minimises these charges before opening an account.

MANAGING YOUR ACCOUNTS

There are a number of useful techniques you can use to reduce your charges and increase the amount of interest you receive. In summary, these include:

Account balancing: It is essential to place your funds where you will be able to minimise interest and charges payable *by* you and maximise interest paid *to* you.

Avoid credit card debt by paying off your bills every month if possible.

Transfer extra funds to reduce expensive consumer finance obligations when the rate you pay for the loan is higher than the rate of interest you receive on your deposits, which is basically all the time.

Account consolidation: Some people have too many accounts in too many banks. By consolidating accounts you may be able to obtain a higher interest rate or receive free services.

Automatic paydown: Make sure you have an arrangement in place to pay down your overdrafts and credit card bills without incurring charges. And be sure to check that the bank executes according to your instructions.

Direct debits: Avoid late charges and cheque fees by setting up direct debits for regular payments such as credit card balances, utility and telecom fees. A regular direct debit to a charity can also be an easy option to allow you to fulfil your philanthropic desires.

Direct debits can make your accounting and expense tracking even easier.

Keeping track of fees and charges: As mentioned in Chapter 13: Credit Cards and Consumer Finance, all account holders should read and check financial statements for accuracy. These statements show when you are charged annual account fees, handling fees, administration fees and other such items.

Your own Wealth Wisdom Plan and Monthly Budget Tracker will keep you well on top of your cash management plans.

It might help to think of managing your cash as a battle for the maximum benefits to be earned from your accounts. As in every battle, make sure you understand the tactical options open to you and make sure you have a strategy to win.

⚮ 21 ⚮

YOUR OWN BUSINESS

Many great American fortunes have been founded on the ownership and development of a single business. For Rockefeller it was oil. Andrew Carnegie's fortune was founded in steel. Bill Gates founded Microsoft and his friend Warren Buffett has built the investment company Berkshire Hathaway with extraordinary success.

Whether you are a tycoon with astronomical wealth or the proprietor of a business of more modest proportions, whether you have built, inherited or purchased your own business, much of your time will appropriately be spent looking after these assets.

For most entrepreneurs and owners of private businesses, the greatest source of future wealth lies in the effective management of their existing business assets. Unless, or until that business is sold, great attention and care should be paid to the protection, development and increased value of your business assets.

HAVE A STRATEGY

As with a Wealth Wisdom Plan, the most important element in business success is having a clear strategy. This means knowing your market, understanding who your customers are and where you will make money. Listening to your customers can help your business to be as successful in the future as it has been in the past, or even more so. More than 80% of business learning takes place in interaction with customers.

Business strategy is not an easy subject, nor one which can be fitted into a brief paragraph or two. If you would like to know more about how to complete a business strategy, you can read Mark Daniell's book *STRATEGY: A Step-by-Step Guide to the Development and Presentation of World-Class Business Strategy* (Palgrave Macmillan 2004). This book gives you a full set of instructions on how to create a valuable strategy for your own business.

SET PRECISE FINANCIAL GOALS

As part of this business strategy, and in coordination with your wealth management plan, you should establish a set of precise goals. This is important to see what salary, dividends or sales value you plan to obtain for your business which will feed into your personal Wealth Wisdom Plan.

Both the income and asset value will play an important role in developing your own wealth, so be sure that your personal goals and business plans are in full alignment. Be sure to determine carefully when and how much money you need to borrow for your business, as this can also have effects on your personal Wealth Wisdom Plan.

BUILD YOUR TEAM

There are two reasons to build a strong team in your business.

The first is to maximise the cash flow, earnings and growth potential of the business. The second is to make sure that there is a team that can carry on the business and protect your investment if something happens to you or one of your key colleagues.

Having a strong and loyal team can be a good form of risk management in any business, as well as a source of high performance and competitive advantage.

FOCUS ON THE CORE

The greatest mistake made by many smart managers is to abandon a successful core business too soon for more glamorous pursuits in new pastures. There is almost always greater potential within your existing business lines, customer relationships and service opportunities than there is in new, untested ventures.

This is not to discourage experimentation and creativity, but to remind us that growth initiatives away from our core clients, markets and existing know-how do have a high failure rate.

A second caveat on growth is to be careful of joint ventures and acquisitions. The failure rate in either one is well above 50%.

If you are planning on gambling on an acquisition, or partnering with a business someone else has built, be very careful to ensure you have done everything possible to beat the dismal odds of success.

Know when to Get Out

One of the hardest decisions for the owner of a family business is to know when to sell. Not all businesses will last forever. Smart entrepreneurs and business inheritors will, after taking careful advice, be prepared to sell at the right price and move on at the right time.

Far too often a founder gets attached to a business almost as if it were a child or spouse, making it difficult to sell even when in decline. Preparing owners of businesses to sell and ensuring that they are fully and properly advised on all aspects of a transaction is one of the most important services that a concerned spouse, family member, friend or adviser can provide.

Think about Leverage

In developing a personal Wealth Wisdom Plan, a business owner may, in some cases, be able to borrow against the assets of his business, commonly know as 'leveraging' his business assets. Borrowing is known as leverage since it can work like a lever to lift the return on equity in a given investment. It should be remembered that adding debt to your business may stretch the equity and equity return a bit further but also it increases the risk of the investment — if things go wrong you will have to pay off all of the debt before you can recover anything for your equity investment.

Leverage may also allow you to reduce risk by using the borrowed money to diversify from a single source of wealth and income. The borrowed fund approach can provide liquidity for purchases of property, pay for educational expenses or provide funding for other investments desired by the business owner. Excess leverage, on the other hand, can crush a business which is operating on thin profit margins or is particularly vulnerable to economic cycles.

Make sure that you put as much thought into your business strategy as you do your Wealth Wisdom exercise in order to maximise the return on equity in your business without jeopardising what could be your greatest current and future asset.

INTEGRATING BUSINESS ASSETS WITH WEALTH MANAGEMENT

Our business success and the creation of our personal wealth are directly linked. To maximise one usually means maximising the other.

It is important to align our business and wealth management plans so that there is an appropriate amount of asset diversification, a coordinated plan for the investment of business proceeds, and no conflicting or excessive demands placed on the funds available.

For some individuals, for whom an owned business is at the heart of a personal wealth plan, more than one discussion needs to take place on how to integrate business strategy with personal wealth maximisation.

UNDERSTAND HISTORY

There are two facts worth remembering when you think about the future of your own family business.

The first is that relationships between management, family and business will evolve over time. In the founding generation of the business, family, business ownership and business management are all rolled into one. By the third generation, family, business ownership and business management have usually moved into separate circles with little overlap other than at the ownership level.

It is important to keep business and personal matters apart as much as possible. It is possible to fire incompetent or unwilling employees; it is much more difficult to fire an underperforming brother or sister.

As INSEAD professor Phil Anderson points out, conduct yourself as if you were a shareholder of a publicly listed company. Have an annual meeting with yourself and ask yourself if everything is in order, if all the paperwork is ok, and, if given the choice, would you actually buy this business today?

The second fact is that only one in seven family businesses survives through three generations. The expression 'riches to rags in three generations' is found in almost every language and culture in the world.

Almost always, the unique family character of a business is both the source of its initial success and the cause of its eventual demise. Perhaps the most valuable decision a family can make is to step back at the right time and to hire high-quality outside professionals to lead the management team. This key decision would allow the family, business ownership and business management spheres to move apart and to seek excellence in their different areas of activity.

❦ 22 ❦

SHARES

A stock or share, essentially the same thing, represents partial ownership — or a share — of a business. The total set of shareholders of any business make up the total ownership of that business.

Developed in Renaissance times to distribute the risk of a ship's trading journey to and from Italy, the idea of dividing up ownership into shares, capable of being bought and sold separately, has been with us for centuries.

Massive technology platforms in New York, London, Tokyo, Hong Kong, Singapore and in many other major cities allow individuals, corporations, pension funds and insurance companies to buy and sell shares around the clock.

ROLE OF EQUITIES

Shares play an important role in almost every investment portfolio, either by allocating a portion of funds directly to a certain company's shares, through investment in a mutual fund, through a hedge fund that acquires shares as part of its strategy, or even through purchasing an insurance policy with an investment element, since that investment will almost always have a large equity component to it.

All equities come with a higher degree of risk than a savings account or a certificate of deposit. They can play many different roles in a portfolio, according to the share selected and the time frame you plan to hold the investment. Unlike long-term certificates of deposit and private equity funds, shares are generally 'liquid', with the owner of the share able to sell within a day or two and turn his or her investment into cash.

Over the long run, shares have offered investors a return superior to bonds or other less volatile investments. But to benefit from that return, investors had to endure the anxiety of some swings, down as well as up, in the stock market along the way.

Because of these ups and downs, which reflect the high volatility of equities, you should take sound professional advice before investing in shares so you can understand the full risks of your proposed investment.

OWNERSHIP OBJECTIVES

Before purchasing any shares, directly or through a mutual fund or an insurance policy, it is important to establish your ownership objectives.

Shares may be purchased for income (achieved through acquiring shares that pay a high dividend), unexploited value (value not yet realised by the market which can make the share price go up when fully understood), capital growth (shares paying low or no dividends but expected to grow in value as the company grows) or other reasons such as portfolio balance or exposure to a foreign currency.

Shares of public listed companies are usually divided into 'growth', 'yield', 'value' and 'blend' categories to fulfil different investment objectives. Growth shares are those which provide growth in revenues, profits and capital value. They may not pay much of a dividend since cash is needed by the company to fuel its growth plans. A yield share is one which is purchased for a relatively large dividend, paid out once or twice a year, which provides a high cash return to the investor. A value share is one which is undervalued by the market but has sound operating characteristics and is seen to have a good future. A blend share is one which combines more than one of these attributes in an attractive blended return for investors.

Types of Shares

Large cap shares: These are shares issued by big companies, usually defined as having sales exceeding US$10 billion per year. They are called 'large caps' because they have a relatively large value in the stock markets as well: 'Cap' stands for 'capitalisation' and means the total value of all the shares in a given company, at a given price, at a given time. Thus the current equity market capitalisation of a business equates to the number of shares outstanding multiplied by the individual share price. A company with one million shares issued which trade at $2 per share, has an equity market capitalisation of $2 million.

In general, bigger companies are seen to be more stable than smaller companies over the shorter term. Big companies are more likely to have a broader base of customers, products and markets. Their management teams are less likely to be dependent upon a few individuals and their operating history gives them a greater chance of continuity into the future.

Small cap shares: As their name suggests, small cap shares are shares issued by smaller companies. Small cap shares may be more volatile than large cap shares. Smaller companies may have greater growth potential than bigger companies and hence greater value growth potential, but these smaller companies may also be less well understood (there will probably be less research available) and have a shorter track record on a listed exchange than many larger companies. Smaller companies may also have a more limited product and/or market base and hence carry more operational risk than a larger and more broadly-based corporation.

Emerging market shares: Even more volatile than small caps are shares listed on emerging markets. Great changes in share value, both up and down, have been observed in Brazil, Russia, India, China (known collectively as the 'BRIC' markets because of their initials) and in many other developing markets.

Many of these markets rise and fall based upon the influx and exit of foreign portfolio investors, who base their investment decisions on broad factors surrounding that market and its currency value. Over the past few years, most Asian markets have been driven, in part, by the inflows (positive impact on the market as demand is higher) and outflows (negative impact) of foreign money.

This greater degree of risk and volatility is one of the reasons emerging market shares can provide, at the right time, greater than average returns or losses to investors.

IPOs: IPO stands for Initial Public Offering of shares, i.e. shares which are being listed on a market for the first time. As a result, IPOs are riskier than shares with a longer trading history. IPOs have no equity market trading history and advisers to the issuing company can only estimate what the correct price for the new share should be. Initial reactions to the new shares can be more positive or negative than professional advisers estimated. IPO shares can move up or down dramatically on the first day of trading.

For a long time, Chinese IPOs were consistently positive in result, as were UK and Malaysian privatisation IPOs and telecoms IPOs in many countries around the world. But other IPO shares have dropped in value immediately upon listing, causing their investors to lose substantial sums of money in a very short period of time.

Index funds: Some investors do not want to take the risk associated with an individual stock but want an investment that will rise (or fall) with the overall equity market. For these investors, investment banks and brokerage houses have set up 'index funds'. These funds are made up of a collection of many shares that rises or falls in line with the market.

Unlike individual shares, these funds are assembled as a collection of representative share investments to reflect the performance of an overall market. So if the New York Stock Exchange goes up by an average of 10%, even though the values of some individual shares within the exchange go up or down a lot more than this average, an index fund goes up 10%. If the market goes down by an average of 5% so does the index fund, regardless of the performance of any one share within the market.

These funds remove some of the risk associated with an individual share and hence reduce the potential return as well.

EQUITY ANALYSTS

Researching a company you may want to invest in takes work. It means reading the annual accounts and following the events surrounding a company and the markets in which it operates. You can also attend the company's annual general meeting, where you can meet the directors and management and assess how capable you think they are.

In addition to these activities, you can examine equity analyst reports on a company. Equity analysts, traditionally employed by brokerage houses and investment banks, are trained to analyse companies and write reports on their findings. These reports cover financial results, future prospects, amount of leverage, competitive momentum, takeover potential (which pushes the price up fast), customer and market prospects, product or service successes and failures, strategic issues, management team strength and other elements of a company's performance. The reports are often based, in part, on interviews with management. They usually contain an estimate of the future value range of the share in the market in which it trades.

Reports conclude with a recommendation to 'buy', 'accumulate', 'hold' or 'sell' a share at the current market price. This recommendation is based on the difference between the analyst's view of the correct share price compared to the current price in the market.

These recommendations should only be taken into account as part of your own investment decision, but the reports are valuable to help improve your understanding of the company. You can get equity analyst reports from your investment adviser, broker or, in some cases, over the internet.

PICKING STOCKS

It is true that many investment brokers fail to add value to the portfolios they manage. On the other hand, there are a few investors and fund managers with a proven approach who beat the market year after year. Warren Buffett, the master of value investing, enunciated his famous two rules of investing, which are well worth remembering:

Rule Number One: Don't lose money.
Rule Number Two: Remember Rule Number One.

In addition to these two general rules, Buffett's investments reflected a consistent philosophy which included:

- Invest in companies you understand.
- Make fewer, better investments.
- Look for strong cash flow and a strong management team.
- Hold for the long term.

Another great investment guru, Benjamin Graham, reputed to be one of Warren Buffett's inspirations, invested only in companies that met a number of criteria including earnings growth of at least 33% per year over 10 years, price-earnings ratio (current share price divided by current earnings per share) below 15 and uninterrupted dividends over 20 years.

According to Pat Dorsey, Director of Stock Analysis at Morningstar, there are five rules for successful investing and seven traps to avoid when buying a share. This approach is described in more detail in *The Five Rules for Successful Stock Investing: Morningstar's Guide to Building Wealth and Winning in the Market* (pp 2 and 13-14).

The five rules are:

- Do your homework — work hard to understand what a company is worth.
- Find economic moats — sources of competitive advantage that protect a business.
- Have a margin of safety — be realistic about current value versus the potential.
- Hold for the long haul — don't try to make a quick buck.

- Know when to sell — holding on to favourite stocks too long can kill your return.

The seven traps are:

- Swinging for the fences — trying to hit a home run every time.
- Believing that it's different this time.
- Falling in love with products.
- Panicking when the market is down.
- Trying to time the markets.
- Ignoring valuation.
- Relying on earnings for the whole story.

These investor 'secrets' have been analysed and broadcast by academics and journalists for years. The answer to successful investing seems to come down to an analytical base leading to a very disciplined approach, avoiding the mistakes of holding on to losses for too long and managing as much risk out of your investment decision as possible.

A Hybrid Approach

Another approach consists of a combination of strategies: Buy index funds for efficient (developed) markets, find a well placed broker in inefficient (developing) markets and buy when there is a major crisis that will have a short recovery period (based on the theory that markets tend to overreact).

There are as many other models for share investment as there are individuals investing in shares. Whatever your chosen approach, it is wise to learn from professionals and to rely on sound professional advice before making any investment.

❦ 23 ❧

BONDS AND MONEY MARKET INSTRUMENTS

A bond is a form of loan taken out by a government or a company. A money market instrument is also a loan to be repaid, with the difference being that a bond is a debt outstanding for a longer period than a money market instrument.

A bond is also a kind of binding pledge or promise, as in the old expression "a man's word is his bond", meaning that any promise made would be honoured. A financial bond is thus a financial obligation to be repaid at a future date, with interest payments and other terms and conditions applying until the loan is repaid.

When governments want to raise money to pay for their various programmes, they can tax their citizens, borrow from banks, or go to the capital markets and issue a bond. A bond is like a giant IOU that pays interest on a regular basis to the investors (people, insurance companies, pension funds) who provide the money to the government. These government-issued IOUs are called government bonds, or 'sovereign' bonds.

When businesses want to raise money, they may borrow from the bank, issue shares to investors in return for new money or issue bonds themselves. These bonds also are sold to the same type of investors as government bonds and pay out a regular interest payment to investors.

Bonds are issued for a set period of time before they 'mature', or fall due for repayment. This maturity date is the time at which the investors will (hopefully) get back the capital they loaned to the business. This may be many years after the date the bonds were issued. The bond 'matures' on a given date, at which point the capital amount borrowed is paid back or 'redeemed' by the government or company who issued the bond.

Bonds usually have a set interest rate (although a few have a 'floating rate' which changes with market interest rates) and thus most will pay out an easily calculated amount at regular intervals, usually twice per year.

Although bonds have a 'face value', often US$1,000 in the US markets, that represents the amount which is to be paid back to the investor at the end of the period, bonds trade at different prices than the face value. The difference results, in part, from changes in market interest rates and changes in the perceived risk that the company — or even a government — will 'default' on the bond, refusing to pay back the amount owed. If the company or government which issued the bond fails to pay back the entire amount borrowed, but does pay back some of the money it borrowed through the bond issue, this is called a 'partial default'.

Role of Bonds

Perhaps the most important characteristic of bonds is that, unlike shares, they pay out a regular income to investors, who are also called 'bondholders'. As sources of income, and often seen as lower risk than shares, bonds and money market instruments play an important role in asset allocation models (see Chapter 18) and can make up a large component of a conservative or income-focused portfolio of investments.

A bond is often purchased for the steady income stream it provides. As a result, they are considered as 'fixed income' instruments, since the interest rate is fixed and paid out on a regular basis.

Bonds are not fixed in price, however. Prices can go up or down over the life of a bond, due to factors related to the company (risk) and markets (primarily interest rates). The price of a bond traded in the market can thus provide capital gain or loss as market interest rates go up and down, just like shares in a company.

When interest rates go up, company profits go down since companies have to pay more to service the same amount of corporate debt. When interest rates go down, the same companies have to pay less in interest costs to service their debt and hence profits – and share prices – tend to go up.

This is the same phenomenon we see in the property market. When mortgage rates go up, house prices tend to go down (or at least go up less quickly) and when interest rates go down, house prices go up (or decline less quickly).

Bonds work the same way. When interest rates go up, bonds with a fixed yield become less attractive relative to the new market prices and their value goes down. When interest rates fall, there is more demand for higher yielding bonds and hence price increases to reflect the increased demand.

A Language all of Its Own

Some of the language used in the bond market still reflects the early days of its conception. A payment to the owner of the bond (who may be the original purchaser or someone who bought the bond in the market, since bonds can be bought and sold like shares) is called a 'coupon' since early bonds had little coupons attached which would be torn off and traded in by the investor for cash at a bank or brokerage house. Even though no one tears off little bits of paper anymore, the term has remained and the electronic payment received by investors in bonds is still called a coupon.

Since whole integer interest rates like 1%, 2%, or 3% are too crude to reflect the subtle changes in such a refined market, dealers and issuers talk about 'basis points' (also called 'bips') which are 1/100 of a percent. So 1% is 100 'bips', 0.5% is 50 'bips' and so on. Even small differences in risk can be captured by the variation of a few 'bips' for purposes of precision in pricing.

Market interest rates for different future periods form a 'yield curve'. Normally, short-term rates are lower than long-term rates and a curve is produced on a graph which slopes upward (higher interest rates) with an increasing timeframe of the investment; if it is the other way around, with short-term rates higher than long-term rates, the yield curve is 'inverted'. Many analysts say that an inverted yield curve is a sign of coming economic difficulties, since it shows that demand for longer-term borrowings is weaker than the shorter-term demand. This means that businesses may be getting more conservative in the expectation of tougher times in the future than they are facing today.

On the other hand, when an inverted yield curve returns to normal, and short-term interest rates are lower than long-term rates again, many observers believe this is a sign of a healthy economy with good growth prospects.

Types of Bonds

Sovereign bonds: One of the biggest bond markets is the government bond market. These are seen as the safest investment around and pay a relatively low interest rate. Government bonds are also called 'sovereign bonds' and are usually issued in the home currency of the issuing government for a large country or in US Dollars for smaller countries.

The US government is considered to have the closest thing to a risk-free status that exists, so US government bonds set the 'risk-free rate' to which other bonds are compared. This also means that the interest you receive as an investor in these bonds is among the lowest in the market.

Some governments, in the past, have defaulted on their bond obligations and left investors with very big losses. It is important to remember that governments, as well as companies, can have some real risk in the bonds they issue.

Municipal and other government bonds: The next category of bonds, which traditionally carry more risk than central government bonds are 'munis', or municipal bonds. In some countries, municipal bonds are exempt from tax, which adds to their attractiveness for investors. There are also bonds issued by states, counties, government organisations, government backed mortgage providers and other administrative agencies.

Corporate bonds: The corporate bond market provides long-term finance to corporations, usually large ones, who wish to avoid the costs, fees and confining terms of a bank loan. Corporate bonds come in almost all currencies, all sizes and with many different yields and durations.

Junk bonds: Technically known as 'non-investment grade' bonds, junk bonds are high risk, pay high interest rates and have relatively little security. Despite the risks of junk bonds, they have been successfully issued by corporate raiders to top up the amount of money they can borrow to buy a target company. Even some once blue-chip companies, due to poor performance, litigation or other problems, have been known to fall on hard times and see their ratings slip from investment grade to non-investment grade as the risk increases of non-payment of the full face value of their bonds.

Yankees bonds, dragons bonds and others: Bonds can be issued in a country other than the one where the originating entity (bank, corporation, government) is situated. Such bonds are called 'foreign bonds' and can be divided into various categories. A 'yankee bond' is a US Dollar-denominated bond issued by a foreign bank, company or government in the USA. If a bond is issued by a foreign entity in Asia and denominated in US Dollars, it is called a 'dragon bond'. If a bond is issued in Japan and denominated in Japanese Yen, the bond is called a 'samurai bond'. A bond issued by a foreign bank, corporation or government in the UK and denominated in British Pounds is a 'bulldog bond'. A 'matilda bond' is the equivalent for bonds issued by foreign entities in Australia which are denominated in Australian Dollars.

Islamic bonds: Not all bonds pay interest to their investors. Islamic bonds — so called because they are created according to Islamic banking principles — pay back their investors based on a non-interest return basis. For example a bond's yield could have come from a share of the revenues from a toll road or other such source of non-interest-based income.

Zero coupon bonds: Zero coupon bonds do not pay interest either, but work on an interest-based calculation. A zero coupon bond is sold at a big discount to its face value and hence grows in value until maturity, at which time the issuing company will pay back the owner of the bond a lot more than it received from the investor when the bond was sold. The increase in value replaces interest as a form of payment for the loan.

For example, a long-term zero coupon bond with a future value of $100 could be sold today for $50. The owner would not receive any interest payments — thus allowing the company to keep its cash for other purposes – but would see the bond grow in value until it matured and the $100 paid out. So the $50 would turn into $100 over time and the owner would be paid in one big chunk at the end instead of lots of little payments along the way and a smaller lump sum at the end. Since there are no interim payments, the 'coupon' is zero and hence the name of 'zero coupon' bond.

Convertible bonds: Bonds can carry other additional features. Some can be redeemed at any time; others can be converted at a set rate into ordinary shares of a business. These are called 'convertible bonds' since they receive interest like a bond and can also be converted into shares when the bondholder chooses.

RATINGS

Since the coupon, or interest rate, of each bond is clearly stated, the most important element in determining the value (and therefore the price) of a bond is the risk element. In the bond world, the risk element is captured in a rating for the bond. These ratings are given like school grades, with AAA at the top.

Needless to say, the higher the risk (and thus the lower the rating) the more a bond issuer is going to have to pay to get investors to buy the bonds.

Three agencies dominate the landscape to rate the risk associated with a particular bond. Based upon a detailed assessment of the issuing company's financial strength, business history, management quality, corporate governance and other factors, these three big rating companies – Moody's, Standard & Poor's and Fitch – give a rating to each bond and company.

Everyone who issues a bond gets a rating from these agencies. In order to rate sovereign bonds, even countries get ratings from these agencies. The risk rating can make an enormous difference to how much that country has to pay to borrow money.

MONEY MARKETS

Although similar in many other ways to bond markets, money markets offer short-term financial instruments in which you can invest.

Money market products have names like 'treasury bills' and 'commercial paper'. Treasury bills are government IOUs with a less than one year maturity. Commercial paper matures in less than nine months (270 days), reflecting the length of maturity at which debt issuers need to register their securities with the Securities and Exchange Commission, the powerful market regulator in the USA. By issuing IOUs for a period of less than 270 days, issuers can avoid the costs and limitations of SEC registration.

Money markets boomed in the USA in the mid-1980s when individuals were allowed to purchase money market certificates and earn a much higher interest rate than they could on regular savings accounts.

Sweep accounts: A sweep account is one which automatically takes the balance of your account (over a predetermined amount) and places it in the money market for you. This avoids your having excessive amounts of money in non-interest-bearing accounts like a checking account.

HOW TO INVEST

There are as many ways to invest in bonds as there are to invest in shares. You can buy an individual bond, just as you can buy an individual share. You can buy an index fund, which reflects the performance of a whole market. You can buy a bond or money market fund, which captures a number of bonds within a single pool.

The different approaches have different risk and return characteristics and different fees attached.

Just as for shares or any other investment, it is important to take high-quality financial advice before deciding to venture forward into any of these investment opportunities.

❧ 24 ❧

MUTUAL FUNDS

For many individual investors, acquiring mutual funds is an easier way to develop a broad portfolio of shares than picking a lot of individual shares by themselves.

A mutual fund or unit trust is a collective investment approach whereby a fund manager buys a portfolio of shares with a common theme on behalf of investors. The difference between a mutual fund and a unit trust is purely a legal difference — one is legally a fund and the other a trust — but they operate the same way from an investor's perspective.

Once the mutual fund (or unit trust) is set up, investors are free to buy and sell shares in the mutual fund as they go along, thus preserving liquidity (the ability to sell an investment on short notice and realise cash) and, historically, providing less risk (because of a more diverse set of and, historically, providing less risk (because of a more diverse set of holdings) — a common investment theme (for example by investing only in small cap growth companies) — and superior returns over time when compared to savings accounts or money market certificates.

Although most mutual fund shares can be sold for cash with little notice, this form of investment is riskier than savings. You can lose some of the value of your capital if the market drops or if the mutual fund you select does not choose its portfolio of shares wisely.

Mutual funds or unit trusts are seen by many people — especially those not familiar with the details of individual share valuation models, asset allocation approaches or brokerage commission schemes — to be a relatively hassle-free way of taking a diversified position in the stock market.

HOW DOES A MUTUAL FUND WORK?

When you buy shares in a mutual fund or unit trust, you are actually buying a tiny percentage of the full range of shares owned by that particular fund or unit trust.

Mutual funds and unit trusts are run by professional managers who define a theme for each portfolio and then select appropriate shares to fit that theme. This allows you to focus on a professionally selected group of shares with a common theme, requiring only a small investment and relatively little effort on your part.

By participating in a portfolio of shares with a common theme, you are able to invest in line with a specific investment goal — for example capital growth or high income — without having to analyse a wide range of individual shares. In addition to making life easier on the analytical front, mutual funds allow you to reduce your risk through a more diversified holding than you would be likely to achieve on your own.

There are three main groups of mutual funds: share funds, bond funds and money market funds, plus numerous subcategories under each heading.

DISCIPLINED PLAN ESSENTIAL

When considering mutual funds, as for any investment consideration, it is important to understand *why* you want to participate in this type of investment before starting to think about how much to invest and with whom to place your money.

HOW SHOULD I CHOOSE THE BEST FUND?

Given the vast range of mutual funds out there, it might seem even more complicated to choose a good fund than to pick a good share. Even if you have set your investment objective of, say, an equal balance of small cap growth and large cap value shares, how can you select the fund most likely to help you achieve your objective?

While there is indeed a large choice, there are a number of ways to make it easier for you to select a mutual fund or unit trust:

Purchase through a reputed fund manager: Fidelity is probably the best known US fund management company and they, along with other large companies of similar reputation, have many high-quality professionals on their staff.

Go to a trusted financial adviser or broker: These trained professionals should have a flow of information allowing them to understand the quality and historic performance of a range of funds. They are able to advise you on the most appropriate fund or set of funds to meet your investment objectives.

Check the ratings: In much the same way as Standard & Poor's or Moody's provide bond and credit ratings on companies, and even countries, a company called Morningstar provides ratings on mutual funds. Morningstar's system rates funds from zero to five stars.

Among other systematic analytical tools, Morningstar uses a 'style box' to describe and analyse a fund's likely performance and role in an investment portfolio. The style box integrates the level of risk (ranked high, medium or low), the investment style (focus on value, growth or a blend) and the average market capitalization (the size of the companies in which the fund invests).

Understanding the rating system and its application to your mutual fund selection may be a helpful tool but it is no guarantee of success. Like a five star hotel, even highly rated funds can experience a decline in performance or sometimes fail to live up to their past reputations.

Read the reports: Ever since the US stock market crash of 1929, mutual funds have had to issue annual reports just as companies do. In these reports, you can find very useful information on the team, the investment philosophy, the track record and the holdings of the fund. These reports should be carefully read and fully understood by you *before* investing in a fund.

It is important to remember that you are responsible for your own investments — and should fully understand and are in control of any investment decision you make.

DON'T TRY TO TIME THE MARKET

It is always tempting to try to time the market, or hold off investing until the market takes a turn for the worse and shares, and therefore mutual funds, are cheaper.

An enormous amount of analysis over many decades of market performance proves that this is not an effective strategy.

It is better to set aside regular amounts of money on a regular basis and invest as and when your investment plan indicates you should to achieve your long-term investment goals.

FEES

Management fees for mutual funds are not low and should be taken into account when assessing the value of your investment.

CONSIDER THE ALTERNATIVES

For the more sophisticated investor, alternatives to mutual funds such as index and tracker funds (being essentially the same) may play the same role in a portfolio, but at lower cost. An index or tracker fund manages a portfolio of shares to match the performance of an overall market. The management component of such a fund is relatively low since the allocations, buying and selling are, in part, done through an automated approach.

As a result, the fees associated with such funds can be significantly lower than for mutual funds, but these funds do require more understanding and management expertise.

REGULAR REVIEW

Although not reviewed as frequently as a portfolio of individual shares, your selection of mutual funds should be reviewed regularly to confirm the fit with your overall investment objectives, to assess performance and to change if you are unsatisfied with your results.

NOT A PERFECT WORLD

As with any class of assets, there are problems that can arise with mutual funds. In 2003, investigations in the USA uncovered widespread inappropriate practices in the mutual fund world. The heads of some of the leading fund companies had to be replaced and market practices improved.

These mutual fund scandals provide more proof of the need and value of a balanced approach to investing.

❧ 25 ❧

PENSIONS

Pensions are an essential part of our retirement planning. Once income from our full time jobs stops, we will need to have a regular flow of income to sustain ourselves and our families. For most people, this will come from one (or perhaps more than one) pension scheme into which we have been paying during our working lives.

Essentially, there are three types of pensions which can support us in our older years: national (or public) pensions, company pensions and private pensions. Each of these three areas will have different characteristics, but all three will need to be considered in your Wealth Wisdom Plan to ensure that you are well taken care of in the future.

Unfortunately, the world of pensions is less solid than it once was. Many governments are not, in fact, putting pension payments into dedicated accounts, but are using current pension contributions to make payments to existing retirees (in some European countries, for example). The beneficiaries of this kind of 'pay as you go' pension system will have to face the possibility of reduced payments in a future when the number of retirees outnumbers the working population.

This dangerous 'pay as you go mode' is not the case in Singapore, for example, where CPF contributions go into a dedicated account in the name of the contributor.

Company pensions may be under-funded (which means that not enough money has been paid in by the company to cover future needs of the pension beneficiaries) and stretched as their beneficiaries grow in number, live longer and use up more pension fund money on increasingly expensive medical care.

Private pension funds, which can act as a top-up or even as a basic income guarantee, need to be run by reliable and solid professionals to ensure that the income produced can live up to the expectations of their members.

In all cases, it is an essential part of a Wealth Wisdom Plan to take a hard-eyed look at your pensions to estimate what they will be able to pay out in the future and what you will need to do to counterbalance any expected shortfall.

NATIONAL PENSIONS

The value of your national pension scheme will vary enormously by the country in which you live and the amount you have paid into the scheme over the years. Current retirees and older members of the workforce may get more benefits than younger people just entering the workforce. Although we would all like someone else to take care of all of our needs, even governments can make mistakes with regard to future pension needs. Alternatively, we may just want more money in retirement than our governments can afford to give.

In any case, we should all take an independent view as to what we can expect from our national pensions and build our own, perhaps more conservative, assessment of future income expectations from national pension schemes into our financial plans.

COMPANY PENSIONS

Over the years, we may have paid into a company pension scheme, or more than one company scheme, to provide for our retirement. It is essential, when taking up a job, to understand what the pension benefits are, whether they can be transferred, and how they are affected by changing jobs, early retirement, layoff or other change in the status quo.

By gathering the right information and from soliciting informed professional views, we can develop a reliable plan for our future using an accurate assessment of our pension plan contributions to our retirement.

PRIVATE PENSIONS

Private pensions may or may not be needed. Based upon the benefits you can expect from your national and company pensions, coupled with any other income you may be able to count on from fixed income or other financial investments, you may want to set aside more money in a private pension to generate a greater flow of income at a later date.

A professional adviser can help to select the best way to save and invest through a private pension, and also help to define the amount you may want to set aside.

ANNUITY

If you want to set aside money today to fund a flow of income in the future, you may want to purchase an annuity. An annuity is an investment which is bought now for a lump sum or purchased through a series of regular payments and then pays out a guaranteed income over an extended time — perhaps even for the rest of your life — from a set date in the future.

The earlier you purchase the annuity and the larger your investment, the larger the income you will benefit from in the future.

Some pension funds can be used to purchase annuities, ensuring a pre-determined amount of income in the future.

Alternatives will vary by country and will be familiar to your adviser or financial planner. You should discuss alternatives with your adviser and decide on an investment in an annuity only after fully understanding the risks and benefits of each product in the context of your overall Wealth Wisdom Plan.

KEY FORMULA

As we have stated already, it may be very valuable to change around the traditional way of looking at personal finances and think about your plans as:

Income minus savings equals expenses

One of the key uses for your savings and investment money can be a well-managed pension plan. By setting aside enough money early on, and adjusting your current expenses to ensure that your future is secure, you will be able to look forward to a comfortable retirement without anxiety or concern.

SAVE EARLY FOR RETIREMENT

The benefits of early saving have also been mentioned throughout the book. If enough is set aside in the early years before the expenses of a family kick in, the demands on a family budget can be less heavy in later years and the amount built up for retirement increased.

By developing and implementing a financial plan which incorporates these two elements — adequate allocation of income to savings and an early start to savings — you will be able to fund a pension plan or other retirement scheme which will pay back through the later years of your life.

PENSIONS FOR WOMEN

When planning pensions, and also when thinking through insurance needs, particular focus has to be put on women. Life expectancy for women is longer than it is for men but, in many cases, they are not as well informed or involved in the financial plans for their golden years. As a result, many women must depend on their children in their old age. They may not have any independent source of income after their husbands have died.

Working women, on average, still receive lower incomes than men. Very often, women do not save for retirement because traditionally family structures were in place which ensured that they would be cared for.

However, a longer life expectancy, coupled with a lack of pension planning and a change in traditional societal structures can lead to disastrous effects, especially after the death of a spouse.

Family structures have been changing for a variety of reasons: fewer children are born, daughters and daughters-in-law (the traditional caregivers of elderly parents) frequently work, and parents may no longer be welcome to move back in with their children when they reach old age. This may mean that Asian families, and in particular women within those family structures, will need to take more initiative for their own pension planning and their own retirement.

GETTING SMART

Whether male or female, young or old, it is important to understand as much as possible about your retirement programme. Some of the questions you should ask about a private pension (which may also be relevant to company or national pensions) are as follows:

- How long will I continue to work?
- How much income will I need after I retire?
- Who will need to live off the pension payments?
- What sources of income will be available from non-pension investments for my retirement?
- What expenses will be covered by a national scheme, a company pension or a private pension?
- What additional income will be needed to fill the gap between expected pension payments, and future needs?
- Is a private pension a good choice for me?
- What programme and features should I consider?
- Is each pension payment guaranteed? Who guarantees it? Is this reliable?
- What if I change my mind and want to cancel?
- What if I want to retire early?
- What happens if I am disabled or can't make payments from some future date onward?
- Do I need additional insurance just in case?

- Is there any tax benefit from a contribution to a pension programme?
- How can I get more information?

PROFESSIONAL ADVICE

Given the complexity and variety of products available, coupled with the importance of the decision, getting professional advice from more than one source is essential. You may want to see a number of providers of pensions to see what is available, what you need and what you can afford.

To make the task easier, you may want to club together with some friends who are looking at the same issues and see different providers and advisers, comparing notes and conclusions collectively after your meetings. You can learn together and help each other to make the most appropriate decisions given different individual circumstances.

This is not an area where you need to compete. Obtaining the best possible information, choosing the best possible products and implementing the best possible financial plan creates a win/win opportunity for everyone involved.

❧ 26 ❧

FOREIGN CURRENCIES

There are many ways to invest in a foreign currency. You can invest by buying a financial asset such as a share or bond in another currency, or invest in a property or other non-financial asset. You can buy a set amount of a foreign currency, like exchanging your currency at a bank, and deposit your money in a local or foreign bank.

You can take a much riskier position by buying an option to buy or sell foreign currency in the future, an investment which can move up or down dramatically in a short period of time with swings in the underlying currency itself.

Obviously the value of a foreign currency asset can increase as well, doubling the upside if the asset also increases, or offsetting a decline in your asset by appreciation in the currency.

Extra Caution Required

Most people operate within a single currency most of their lives. We receive a salary, pay for our homes and living expenses, educate our children and plan to retire in the same currency. This means that all objectives should be tied back to that currency when making savings and investment decisions.

Participation in a foreign currency investment needs to be made with double caution. You will need to understand both the risks and return potential of the investment and the risks and return potential of the currency.

Role in a Portfolio

Foreign currencies can play many roles in a portfolio.

Diversification: In some countries, there is a limited set of investment alternatives. There may be a particular political risk or economic risk which needs to be taken into account when setting out investment objectives.

When deciding on your own asset allocation, you should be sure to consider the need to diversify away from any one big risk or 'avoid concentration risk' as the experts say.

Speculation: It is hard for a small retail investor to have more knowledge than the currency market experts and consistently make the right call on interest rates, exchange rates or political events. In order to win in forecasting currencies, a great deal of skill and luck is required over the long term.

Hedging: Foreign currency investments can also act as a counterbalance or 'hedge' against some negative events which would damage other investments you hold. This may mean that, if you hold a lot of US Dollar shares, you may want to buy a US Dollar option that will go up in value if the US Dollar drops in value. By purchasing this kind of option, you are protecting the value of your investment in home currency terms.

Matching future expense. If you are planning for an education abroad for your children, it makes sense to look into saving or investing in the currency most relevant for their future education. This could be, for example, the US Dollar, British Pound or Australian Dollar. By setting out your wealth objectives and needs in the most relevant currency, you may find that you have no choice but to have a foreign currency element in your plans.

UNDERSTAND THE POTENTIAL IMPACT

Speculating in foreign currencies, and holding foreign assets such as shares, properties and bonds, doubles your risk exposure.

As an example, investing in a US Dollar share from Singapore, or investing in UK property from Malaysia, means taking on the risk of the US Dollar or British Pound declining in value relative to your own currency. This currency risk is in addition to the risk of the share or property market declining. Even if the share value goes up or the property appreciates, a decline in the value of the dollar or pound against your currency could more than offset your gain.

To take a recent example, houses in the London property market increased 4.9% over the year 2005. On the other hand, if you were investing from Singapore, the British Pound declined 6.5% over the same time frame against the Singapore Dollar. The listed rate fell from S$3.10 to the Pound at the beginning of 2005 to S$2.90 by the end of the year.

So if you had invested $1 million Singapore Dollars in a house in London at the beginning of 2005, this translates into an initial investment of slightly more than £320,000 at the exchange rate of S$3.10 per British Pound prevailing at the beginning of 2005. An average British house would have appreciated by 4.9% over the full year, so the value of your property investment would have risen by 4.9%, to £336,000 at year end. However, due to the decline in value of the British Pound against the Singapore Dollar over the same period, this amount of £336,000 would at the end of the year have been worth only S$970,000 when converted back into Singapore Dollars. Thus, the increase in the London property value would have been more than offset by the decline in the British Pound and you would have lost S$30,000.

If you financed the whole purchase with a Singapore Dollar loan at 5%, you would have had to subtract an interest cost of S$50,000 as well. At the end of the year, the pre-tax *loss* would thus have been around S$80,000 for a UK investment that went up almost 5% in value in local currency terms.

FEWER CURRENCIES

Over recent years, the number of currencies in which one can trade speculatively has reduced dramatically. The elimination of the German Deutschmark, the Italian Lira, the French Franc, the Spanish Peseta and other European national currencies with the arrival of the Euro has wiped out a high degree of market variety.

Today, there are three major currency blocks: the US Dollar, the Euro and the Japanese Yen. They do not move together and any one can rise or fall dramatically against another in a relatively short period of time. Because they reflect the underlying factors of different geographies with different economic policies and prospects, each currency moves separately and each has its own characteristics and chances for long-term appreciation against others. The currencies of other countries also move according to a number of factors, some predictable and others not.

A number of currencies over the past few years have been pegged to the US Dollar or trade within a narrow band around a preset value of the US Dollar. These currencies include, among others, the Hong Kong Dollar, the Chinese Renminbi (much to the dismay of US government officials, who think the Yuan should go up a lot in value to make US goods more competitive) the Malaysian Ringgit and many Middle Eastern currencies.

Other tradable currencies include the British Pound, the Swiss Franc, the Swedish Krona, the Norwegian Krone, the Canadian Dollar and the Australian and New Zealand Dollars, along with a broad selection of emerging market currencies such as the Indian Rupee, the Indonesian Rupiyah, the Thai Baht and many others.

Even with fewer opportunities in which to invest or speculate, the potential role and impact can still be significant in your portfolio. You need to stay on top of the currency markets; the Foreign Exchange Market is now a 24-hour market that never sleeps. It is essential that you understand all aspects of your currency positions if you are not to lose sleep over your investments in a foreign currency.

You will need to make sure you are fully aware of all of the risks as well as the opportunities before you embark on any cross-border or cross-currency investment.

DANGERS OF MISMATCH

By making separate decisions on investments and currency exposure risk, you can avoid the trap into which many businesses fell in Asia in the 1990s when they did not take currency risk seriously enough in their own investment plans.

Too many companies had borrowings (and hence interest payments) in US Dollars and profits in Indonesian Rupiyah or another relatively weak currency. When these weak currencies dropped, the US Dollar interest payments became unsustainable and businesses could no longer pay their debts.

It has taken many years to clean up the mess in the banks and business landscape as a result of this unmanaged currency mismatch.

A personal equivalent to the Asian Economic Crisis would be to have all of your income generating assets in a foreign currency, for example US Dollars, and all of your living expenses in Singapore Dollars. A collapse in the US Dollar — long predicted by famous economists like Jeffrey Sachs and others — would decrease your Singapore Dollar income substantially.

Managing your currency exposure thoughtfully by avoiding a mismatch of assets (in one currency) and liabilities (in another currency) should allow you to avoid a personal economic crisis of the same magnitude as the economic crisis of the last decade.

TREAD CAREFULLY

As with any investment, you should take prior advice from a highly informed investment adviser before speculating on currencies or pursuing any other investment opportunity with a foreign currency angle.

The key insight in analysing investments in which there is a foreign currency exposure is to ensure that you fully understand and accept all of the risks involved and make a separate and informed decision about both the currency exposure and the underlying investment.

❧ 27 ❧

GOLD AND COMMODITIES

Commodities are the basic materials that make up the foundation of the world economy. Oil, natural gas, wheat, rice, sugar, coffee, cocoa, maize, iron ore, live cattle, pork, orange juice, milk, cotton, wool, rubber, gold, copper, nickel, silver and aluminium are the major items traded on the world's commodities exchanges.

Most investors tend to focus on shares rather than commodities. The international media channels have daily shows reviewing the performance of global stock markets, reporting in detail on the earnings announcements, quarterly results and daily moves in the share prices of General Electric, Microsoft, Toyota, Google and other large cap stocks. There is relatively little coverage of the commodities market.

This relatively low interest is surprising because, according to a 2006 report by UBS, the trading volume of the world's commodities markets exceeds that of most global financial markets. This report states that the traded volume in the top 35 commodities alone exceeded $2.2 trillion annually. With oil and gold prices staying at high levels, or even trading higher under certain scenarios, the scale of the markets will remain substantial for many years to come.

As well as the sheer volume of the commodities markets, the products and factors influencing the market such as weather, growth of demand in China and India, and other factors may be more easily understood than those affecting the share markets. Even more importantly, prices have been rising faster in commodities in the new millennium than they have in some stock markets.

OIL AND BEYOND

Of all the commodities traded, oil and energy are by far the largest category. The dynamics of the oil business are a constant presence on the front pages of the world's newspapers. The lack of large new oil discoveries, the accelerating consumption driven by the USA, China and India, price spikes due to major political and economic events, the race to tie up scarce global resources, the massive profits made by a few giant oil companies, periodic petrol station queues and shortages in many countries and subsidies (and their removal) are all reflections of the dynamism and scale of this market.

The impact of high oil prices on other commodities is also unprecedented. A renewed emphasis on bio-fuels and other alternatives to expensive petroleum imports means that high oil prices even increase the price of sugar.

How does this work? Sugar cane and sugar beets are the raw materials refined into sugar. Sugar from either source can be used to produce ethanol. Ethanol can be used as a fuel or fuel additive instead of oil-based products. Fuel prices are driven by oil price. So when the price of oil goes up, the demand for — and price of — sugar also rises as it is an alternative source for consumers.

Although there is a knock-on effect into many other markets, the oil and gas market itself is where the main action takes place. Prices vary enormously, with this volatility creating opportunities for very profitable (or very unprofitable) participation.

Oil prices have gyrated for many years. The all-time high, when looked at in 'constant' dollars, was actually in the 19th century, just before the big Russian discoveries of oil came into the market. Prices in the early 1980s were higher in constant dollars (dollars with the impact of inflation taken out) than they were in the recent period 2004–2005 of high per-barrel prices.

There are many ways to participate in the oil market. Shares in energy companies or energy service companies may be the easiest way to invest. Big oil companies like BP, Shell and Exxon/Mobil have vast reserves as well as refineries, petrol stations and refined products. BP, in particular, is also investing in alternative energy sources.

Investors can also buy energy-related mutual funds, commodity funds, commodity index funds, oil price options (see Chapter 30 for an explanation of options) and other products to participate in the market.

The oil price can also impact other investments. For example, when the oil price goes up, shares in airline companies may go down to reflect the fact that their profits will be reduced because of higher fuel bills.

As a result, it always pays to keep an eye on oil prices and interest rates as they can have an important impact across many parts of a financial plan.

GOLD

After being relatively dormant for a number of years, the price of gold rose dramatically in the new millennium, standing at US$513 at the end of 2005.

Gold has played a unique role in history as the ultimate measure and metaphor of wealth. From the beginning of recorded history and in almost all civilisations, gold has been a symbol of personal riches. The Midas touch, which turned all objects into gold, is still used as the expression to describe someone highly capable of creating great wealth.

In the modern world, gold plays several different roles in an investment portfolio. It is still seen as a safe haven in times of heightened political risk. It is a hedge against inflation and a surrogate international currency. It is a scarce metal which is a key element in jewellery-making for developed and developing markets and a vital industrial input as well.

Gold is not abundant. Despite the thousands of years that it has been used as an international medium of exchange, only around 32,000 tonnes of gold are now in existence at central banks. The new annual production is lagging behind demand at only 2,600 tonnes per year.

Investment opportunities in gold can be found in the substance itself, gold mining company shares and index funds.

OTHER COMMODITIES

Broadly, the world's other commodities fall into two categories, renewables and non-renewables.

Renewables: These are products which can be replaced as they are consumed. This category includes commodities like corn, coffee, sugar, cocoa and other agricultural products. Prices for these 'soft' commodities vary with each crop season. An abundant crop means lower prices because of greater supply. A weak year due, for example, to drought will mean significantly higher prices.

Non-renewables: These are commodities such as iron ore, aluminium and other 'hard' commodities. These products, many of which are extracted from the earth, are not dependent upon weather cycles like the 'softs' mentioned above.

Even though there is no exposure due to weather patterns, 'hard' commodities are driven by supply and demand factors like any other industry. In the case of many commodities, demand from China has created a major increase in prices and volumes. The price of steel, for example – a critical component in the manufacture of cars, trucks, washing machines and other goods – rose more than 150% from the beginning of 2002 to the end of 2005. Iron ore, with the majority of production volumes now in the hands of only four producers, rose at an even faster rate of more than 230% over the same period.

CHINA AND INDIA

The rise of the world's two largest nations to become new powerhouse economies is a factor in recent price increases and in future demand expectations for commodities. Competition for energy resources, textile raw materials and food ingredients for increasingly wealthy populations has led to an expectation of continued demand pressure on almost all commodities for a significant time to come.

RISE IN PERFORMANCE

For many years, commodities were an area of investment that, in the words of commodity guru Jim Rogers, "got no respect".

Seen as complex, volatile and uninteresting, this asset class was not often featured in glamorous news bulletins or taught in business school courses focused on the financial markets.

Recent increases in the value of individual commodities and the newly available commodity index funds are moving the commodity market slowly into the limelight. In 2005, after 25 years as 'poor' asset classes, four of the top six performing index funds were commodity funds.

'NEGATIVE CORRELATION'

One final point in favour of commodities is that they may provide a natural hedge against the US Dollar or stock market exposure some people have in their investments. Since commodities are traded globally, the fact that they are quoted in US Dollars should not mask the fact that they can hedge, to some extent, against a decline in the value of the dollar itself. If the US Dollar plunges in value, the value of commodities on international markets usually rises to compensate for the decline in the US Dollar.

VOLATILE AND COMPLEX MARKETS

Buying oil, gold or other commodity futures on the various commodity exchanges is not a game for beginners, nor for the faint of heart.

There are, however, many other ways to participate in the commodities asset class on a lower risk basis, through commodity funds, index funds and other approaches which could form part of an investment portfolio.

As with all investments, you should consult a professional investment manager before making any investment in commodities.

❧ 28 ❧

ARTS AND ANTIQUES

One of the great benefits of accumulating wealth is the ability to acquire assets that are both aesthetically pleasing and increasing in value at the same time.

Some of the great fortunes of history have been associated with the collection of art and antiques. The Getty Foundation in the USA, the baronial Thyssen-Bornemiszas of Europe and the ruling family of the Principality of Liechtenstein are, or were, all great collectors of art which has skyrocketed in value over time.

Almost everyone collects something, not necessarily as an investment, but because he or she likes the objects themselves. However, these collections may also build up significant value over time.

Paintings, sculptures, furniture, silver, jewellery, vintage cars, wine and many other of the finer things in life are known as 'collectibles' in the wealth management world.

They fall into a wide range of categories, some of the most popular of which are enumerated below. Although the categories differ, there are some common rules to be observed in selecting assets for acquisition in any category.

Understand supply and demand: The first rule is to understand the fundamental drivers of supply and demand for each category. For example, there is a limited supply and an increasing demand for antique Chinese art due to the increasing wealth of the Overseas Chinese and the rise of a wealthy entrepreneurial class in China itself. These two factors — limited supply and increasing demand — provide a healthy foundation for sustainable growth in asset values. The same is true for Indian art as well.

Watch out for theft, fakes and frauds: Sadly, there are many fake items circulating and passed off as genuine in the world of collectibles. Even respected dealers in antiquities have been known to sell stolen items without being aware of their deception, with hard-to-detect fakes and heavily repaired items described as perfect pieces.

The manufacturers of high-quality fakes are getting smarter and more skilled over time; one of their latest tricks is to use old wood, old tools and old techniques to manufacture antiques for sale abroad. These well-crafted pieces are then stained and buried underground for a few months to cover over any sign of recent work. Even the experts can be fooled by such painstaking fraud.

It is very important to know what you are doing in this area and to seek advice from experts. You should deal only with reputable dealers (of which there are far too few) and obtain a certificate of authenticity for each piece you purchase. Learn as much as you can about the asset you are interested in; it is useful to study available books, price guides and articles, to speak to dealers and experts at auction houses, and to visit museums and galleries.

As set out before, Warren Buffett has warned us to observe two rules to be successful in investing:

Rule Number One: Don't lose money.
Rule Number Two: Remember Rule Number One.

These rules are just as valuable in the art world. Make sure that you do not invest in any theoretically valuable antique piece which could, in reality be 'only of decorative value' as the auction house valuers say in their most diplomatic language when faced with a fake or commercially worthless item.

The purchase, even innocent, of stolen pieces of art or pieces of national cultural value removed from a particular country without the requisite permissions could not only result in a total loss of your investment, but also could carry fraud penalties or even a jail term.

In no other domain of your Wealth Wisdom Plan are the words *caveat emptor* — let the buyer beware — more directly applicable.

THE AUCTION HOUSES

One way to purchase pieces that have been reviewed by experts or just to learn about an art category is to attend auctions held by the major international auction houses. The Big Two, Sotheby's and Christie's, travel to all parts of the world with some regularity.

The content of various sales, for example Asian paintings or luxury watches, are shown on a travelling basis in a few major capital cities before auctions are held in London, Hong Kong, New York or Geneva. Although it is usually the multimillion dollar items that capture the headlines, there are also many items priced at a few thousand dollars which may (or may not) increase in value after purchase.

Other auction houses, such as Bonham's in London or International Auctioneers, provide opportunities to purchase items in person or by phone-in participation. Some selected items may also be sold in designated sale rooms outside the traditional auction forum.

As with all asset purchases and sales, agents' commissions must also be taken into consideration. At an auction house, both the buyer and seller may have to pay commissions. The buyer's commission is usually in the region of 20% of the amount bid for the purchase. The seller's commission is about the same. Both buyer and seller pay a significant premium when items are handled by one of the major auction houses. These costs need to be taken into account before venturing forth into the art world.

PASSIONS AND PREJUDICES

When you buy at auction, it is important to set spending limits and to stick to them. All too often, we can get carried away by the prospect of acquiring a nice example of a favourite artist's work and paying way above the true value. This can lead to 'buyer's remorse', the expensive regret of not having been more disciplined at the time of a purchase.

THE ART MARKET IS ON THE RISE

Almost half of all auction sales turnover takes place in the USA and almost three quarters of all auction turnover worldwide comes from paintings. The art market has performed very well recently almost everywhere according to the Art Trends 2005 report.

Asian art, in particular Chinese art, has taken off in recent years. Auction estimates for Asian art are not only being met but, in some case, many times exceeded. Chinese, Japanese, Indian and Vietnamese art is becoming more and more sought after. Contemporary art is also increasingly in demand.

Buyers come from both overseas and local markets, with overseas buyers often searching out items from their own cultural background. Overseas Chinese tend to buy Chinese art and Non-Resident Indians acquire Indian items of various ages.

The art market is generally one you should enter only with a long-term perspective. Art investments are usually illiquid and expensive to buy and sell in the short term.

Popular 'Collectibles'

Detailed below are some of the more popular categories of collectibles you may wish to consider for investment or enjoyment — or both.

Paintings: Both contemporary and antique paintings are sought after for decorative reasons and may also be attractive from an investment perspective. Late 19th century paintings, for example, became well known years ago for their investment value. Huge sums were paid for paintings by French Impressionists, leading to a speculative bubble which was bound to burst — and did in 1990.

Recently, record prices for paintings sold at auctions made the headlines again when 34 paintings, selling for more than US$1 million each, reached a total price of US$120 million in one evening at Sotheby's London sale of Impressionist and Modern Art in February 2006.

Posters and prints: Prints and posters are very attractive to many buyers, in part because they are far less expensive than original paintings. Posters ranging from vintage ski posters to

Andy Warhol posters are particularly sought after, as are selected other prints ranging from 17th century pieces to Miró items.

Photography. Modern and vintage photography has attracted much interest recently, with sales by year end 2005 reaching new heights. In February 2006, a new record was broken by the sale of a photograph (Edward Streichen's The Pond-Moonlight) for almost US$3 million at Sotheby's New York.

Religious items and statues. Religious items have always been revered and have also attracted interest from collectors for centuries. Once again, it is tremendously important to check the provenance of any item you purchase. Cambodia's Angkor Wat has been diminished in its glory by people stealing pieces from the ancient temples, churches in Europe have been robbed of statues and important religious writings have been looted from libraries. The purchase of stolen artefacts can lead to great trouble in the long term as international efforts to recover stolen art increase in intensity.

Furniture and furnishings. Antique, vintage and modern pieces in excellent condition have been increasingly sought after in recent years. Inevitably, Asian furniture is likely to feature more prominently, and at higher prices, in international auctions in coming years.

Jewellery: Jewellery is a broad category which requires particular expertise as there are vast quality differences between pieces, with significant financial implications associated with the differences. It is not easy to gain expertise on jewellery, and one should learn as much as possible about precious gems and jewellery design, before starting to build a collection, and especially before making a big purchase.

Novice investors, in particular, should always buy from a trustworthy source and ask for a certificate stating the quality of the precious stones involved. This is especially true when purchasing a costly item. When buying certain gemstones, it is advisable to check to see if they have been heat-treated and whether such treatment makes a difference in the value of the stone. Some types of gemstones are almost always heat-treated; others are far less valuable when exposed to heat treatment in order to enhance the colour. It is also important to check the setting of the jewellery: Is it designed to hide a flaw in a stone?

Watches: For many people, wearing an expensive watch is a status symbol, similar to owning certain high performance cars. Some people move on to collect enough higher priced items to start off a small watch collection, which may turn into a major passion. Collecting timepieces can be a good investment over time, but only if the quality of the time-pieces is very good and the selection of individual pieces well informed.

Silver: Both as a decorative and useable asset, silver has enjoyed popularity for centuries in Europe, Asia and America. Excellent quality pieces from long-deceased silversmiths come at a hefty price, but they may be a good investment in the long term if the category grows in popularity.

Books and manuscripts: The books and manuscripts market is small but has appreciated rapidly in selected sectors in recent years. Of particular note are examples from the very early days of book printing as well as manuscripts which date back even earlier.

Carpets: Both for Westerners and Asians, carpets are a key part of the history of the decorative arts and may, if carefully selected and maintained, grow in value as well. From antique silk carpets, which can be very precise in their details and very highly priced, to Tibetan prayer carpets, hand-woven carpets from the East have been attractive investments and may well continue to be so in the future.

Vintage automobiles: Vintage automobiles have risen and fallen substantially in value over the years. Proper storage of these vehicles is of utmost importance as rust may develop, especially on older cars which did not have good rust protection at the time of manufacture. Several countries have special provisions for the use of vintage automobiles which allow very limited use at very low tax rates and registration fees. Singapore, for example, has a special road tax rate for cars of at least 35 years of age, provided they are driven for a maximum of 28 days per year.

Wine: Sotheby's estimated that, for the year 2005, the wine sector grew by 40% worldwide. These (in the very literal sense of the word) liquid assets often remain illiquid for a while however, as wines need storage time to mature fully. Storage conditions must be strictly adhered to as an entire investment may become diminished in value if poorly stored.

Other 'collectibles' include sculptures, swords and militaria, stamps (which still account for around 2% of all auction transactions) and antique maps (which are also very much sought after by some investors).

FUNDS

Given the recent interest by some investors in art investments without having to physically buy and store individual pieces, art funds have been created to allow easier investment in the overall art market or in specific segments. Similarly, with the increased interest in wine as a financial investment, wine funds have been launched.

These funds are managed by professionals who oversee acquisition, storage, insurance and sale of selected pieces.

MANAGING YOUR COLLECTION

If you are taking possession of actual items, you will need to be sure that the correct storage or display conditions protect the value of your investment. Wines, paintings, porcelain, cars, statues and other collectibles can be broken, stained, scratched, crashed or otherwise damaged — or even stolen if not properly looked after.

Specially developed computer software is available for the purpose of monitoring the value and location of a collection. Photographs and descriptions of all the items in your collection should be preserved and, if available, evaluation reports as well.

It is also very important to make sure you have sufficient insurance protection to cover any loss of or damage to your collection under the full range of potential risk events. Any additional insurance premiums need to be taken into account when calculating your investment costs.

❧ 29 ❧

PRIVATE EQUITY

Private equity, along with hedge funds, may be the best known asset class within the broader grouping of 'alternative assets'. These assets are categorised as such because they provide an alternative to the traditional capital market classes of stocks, bonds, mutual funds and other products freely traded on the major capital exchanges of the world.

Like hedge funds, private equity is regarded as a product for the sophisticated investor. High risk and illiquid, private equity funds have played an increasingly large role in some of the worlds most sophisticated and successful institutional portfolios, such as those administered for the endowments of Harvard and Yale universities in the USA.

Historically, good private equity funds managed by top quality private equity fund managers such as Bain Capital, Carlyle, Golden Gate, TPG, Kleiner Perkins and others have systematically outperformed the public markets by quite dramatic margins.

What is Private Equity?

Private equity is capital provided as investment in unlisted companies or through privately negotiated transactions with public corporations.

Private equity is provided by individuals, corporate entities or from an increasingly large and powerful set of private equity funds for specific transactions. Many well-known companies are now or have been owned or controlled by private equity corporations, including Burger King, Domino's Pizza, Gucci, the Raffles Hotel Group, Toys R Us and other businesses.

Unlike most investments in publicly listed shares, private equity investments often entail significant investor involvement in the affairs of the business.

Private equity funds, for example, may provide numerous board members, change management teams, reset business strategies, control dividend policies, restructure corporate assets and balance sheets, sell parts of a business, merge with competitors, set new performance targets and, eventually, list or sell the business.

Types of Private Equity

Private equity can take many forms and provides a variety of investment opportunities with different risk/return characteristics.

Private equity funds may focus on a series of deals in specific industrial sectors such as technology, media, healthcare or property. They may also focus on a specific country. The main forms of private equity transactions are explained below.

Seed and venture capital: The capital required to start a business or fund its earliest stages is called seed capital or venture capital. The amounts of money required at this level are usually smaller than those of a more developed business, but the risk of failure is higher. Some enormous successes and spectacular returns have been achieved by seed and venture capital investors, but far more of these investments die an early death, resulting in a total loss of capital invested.

Growth capital: Once a company is up and running, it may need capital to fund its continuing growth.

Companies which have not had time to generate sufficient cash flow may require growth capital to fund their own growth needs. These needs may include infrastructure expansion, team development, R&D and working capital. Growth capital investments are often small and negotiated on a friendly basis with the management team of an unlisted company.

LBOs: A leveraged buyout (LBO) is usually the acquisition of an existing company by an individual or private equity fund using a combination of private equity and a lot of debt: The higher the debt, the greater the leverage on the investment.

Leverage magnifies investment risk. As we have seen earlier, adding debt to the equity paid for an acquisition can change the nature of the investment quite visibly. If a private equity investment of $100 is made to buy a business without using any debt (an unlevered transaction) and the business is then sold for $120, a return of 20% will have been achieved.

On the other hand, if the same business is bought for $100 using $10 of private equity and $90 of borrowed money, and then sold for $120, the return on equity is 200%, as the original $10 would turn into $30 after repayment of the debt (but before taking into account any interest paid to the lender).

Using this same example, a decline in the value of the business would have a dramatically negative impact on return if leveraged. If the business is bought for $100 using $100 of equity and is sold for $90 shortly thereafter, the investor has lost 10% of his or her investment.

On the other hand, if the same business is bought for $100 using $10 of equity and $90 of debt and then sold for $90, all of the sale proceeds will pay off the debt first and the investor, in this instance, would have lost all of the money invested.

MBOs: A management buyout (MBO) is a transaction where the existing management team buys control of the business they operate. Such a transaction can take place with or without a financial partner and with or without leverage in the acquisition capital structure.

BIMBOs: There are lots of variations on buy-ins, buyouts and other private equity transactions. One of these categories goes by the amusing acronym of 'BIMBO' (a Buy in Management Buy Out) where new and existing management and investors take control of a business.

Mezzanine financing: The private equity market uses a variety of structures to fund acquisitions, with differing levels of risk and return.

Of these, senior debt, usually in the form of bank borrowings, has the lowest return but also carries the lowest risk. Senior debt has no capital upside and makes its return from its profit margin on the interest charged. It is paid out before any other class of liability, hence its title.

The highest return, and hence highest risk, is the equity portion of the transaction. Private equity investment can have a huge range of outcomes, from enormous payouts to enormous losses.

In between senior debt and equity, with a medium level of risk and a medium expectation of return, is intermediate, or mezzanine, capital.

Like the half floor its name suggests, mezzanine is usually a smaller element of the capital structure than senior debt. It may have an interest component and carry some capital upside. The return on 'mezz' is paid out after senior debt but before equity.

Junk bond funds, distressed debt funds, vulture funds: These funds focus on investing to make a return on damaged assets, sub-investment grade bonds and other assets where fund managers have found ways to unlock or benefit from value that the market has not seen.

PERFORMANCE

Good private equity funds can return 20-40% per year, and sometimes even more, to their investors. Looking back in time, there are a few observations about private equity performance worth noting.

The first is that private equity funds are like wine: There are good years and bad years. Funds raised at the peak of a share market, for example in 1989 and 2000, have generally had dismal returns.

The second observation about private equity funds also draws a parallel with wine: A few are great and many are mediocre. The majority of private equity funds do not exceed average public market performance in the markets in which they operate.

The strategic imperative for investors is to gain access to the best fund managers if at all possible.

FEES AND 'CARRY'

Most private equity funds managers charge fees to their investors in two different ways: First, an annual management fee is charged, usually 2% of the capital commitments to a fund. Second, a share of the profits from the deals, called the 'carried interest' or 'carry', is charged. This usually amounts to 20% of the profits achieved above a pre-set 'hurdle rate' which recently has been around 8%.

How to Invest

Private equity investments are not easily available to retail investors. Traditionally, private equity investments have been open only to large institutions like insurance companies and pension funds, along with a few high net worth individuals.

For most small investors, the large amounts of money required to participate, the high risks and lack of liquidity make private equity relatively unappealing as a direct investment.

For those interested in participating because of historical high returns, there are a few listed private equity funds and the chance to participate as part of a balanced portfolio run by one of the larger institutions. Professional advice is of importance when contemplating an investment in this area.

❧ 30 ❧

DERIVATIVES, OPTIONS
AND HEDGES

Most of the investments described in the above chapters are pretty straightforward. They describe a range of direct investments in ownership of a business, publicly listed shares in a business, bonds, savings accounts, commodities, art and property.

Other categories describe investments in pools of these same assets, or groups of investments that allow you to spread your risk and achieve a specific portfolio objective. These pooled investments include mutual funds, index funds, commodity funds, private equity funds, insurance policies with investment and pensions.

Each of these investments carries a different risk and return balance and a different fee structure for participation. Most of these products are easily understood and can be chosen by the novice or intermediate investor with a little homework and reading. In addition, almost all of these areas are regulated to provide the retail investor with some degree of protection for his or her assets.

There is another world of investments and participations which are not direct investments or participation in a pool of direct investments. They can be exceedingly volatile, are often unregulated, are most certainly not for a novice investor, and perhaps not even appropriate for an intelligent person with an intermediate knowledge of the markets.

This is the world of derivatives, options and hedges.

WHAT IS A DERIVATIVE?

A derivative, as the name implies, is a financial instrument or investment whose value is derived from another asset, reference rate or index. Many derivatives are linked to the price of a particular commodity, security, bond or currency. The value of the derivative — for example an options contract — goes up or down in relation to the asset, reference rate or index. For example, an option to buy an ounce of gold at today's price will go up or down in the future as the price of gold rises and falls.

Derivatives, unlike the direct investments described above, do not confer ownership of an asset. Derivatives can be, and usually are, traded separately from the underlying asset with which they are linked.

WHAT IS AN OPTION?

An option is a right to buy or sell an investment or asset at a future date. If the option is to buy something, for example a share, it is described as a 'call' option since the ownership of the share can be called in like a loan or other obligation.

If the option is to sell something, it is called a 'put' option, since it gives you the legal right to put something into someone else's hands at a price and on the terms described in an option agreement.

An option differs from a 'forward' or 'forward contract', in which the holder of the contract has a fixed obligation to deliver goods — say a ton of coffee or a share in a particular company — on a specific day at a specific price. An option is just that — you may or may not want to exercise the option and can opt to walk away without obligation if you so choose.

While it is possible to walk away from an option, in so doing you lose the entire price you paid for it. If there is no sale, you will have made a 100% loss on your investment, possibly in a very short period of time.

On the other hand, if you have an option to buy gold at $500 an ounce and the current market price is $800 per ounce, the value of the option would increase significantly in value. The $300 per ounce profit you would make is called the 'intrinsic value' of the option.

Options pricing is complicated and depends upon the nature of the option (for example, is it exercisable only on a set day at the end of a period or can it be exercised at any point during the option period), the length of time for which you hold the option and the volatility of the underlying asset.

The most commonly used method to value options is the Black-Scholes model, which calculates a value based upon the above-mentioned factors. Professors Scholes and Merton won the Nobel Memorial Prize for Economics for their work on options pricing in 1997.

What is a Hedge?

A hedge, either in a particular hedge position or through a hedge fund investment, can play a valuable role in managing risk out of an investment position. A hedge is an investment made to balance another investment. For example, an investor with a big bond portfolio might be worried that interest rates could go up and reduce the value of an investment. So, to 'hedge' the interest rate risk (like the old phrase of 'hedging your bets'), he or she might make an investment that made a profit when interest rates went down.

What is a Hedge Fund?

Traditionally, hedge funds are pools of money, now exceeding US$1 trillion in total, which traded to achieve the specific investment objectives of sophisticated investors, such as providing protection of capital value if the stock market went down or if oil prices went up. Most hedge fund investors in the past were sophisticated investors, including institutions and high net worth individuals. In the past, hedge funds could be used to reduce risk in investment strategies or to balance out risks and exposures in another part of an investor's portfolio.

These days, a large number of hedge funds have raised an enormous amount of money and are looking for any kind of investment remotely near their original mission in which they can make money. Time will soon tell whether there is too much money in hedge funds (many of which should be renamed as 'speculative funds') chasing after too few good opportunities barely within the scope of their mandates.

Weapons of Financial Mass Destruction

Hedge funds and investments in the world of derivatives can have enormous impact on investment portfolios – both good and bad. George Soros and his Quantum Fund made huge profits when they pushed the British Pound out of the European Exchange Rate Mechanism and forced a devaluation which earned them more than US$1 billion in 1992.

The risks of speculation in derivatives are high and huge losses are also possible. Orange County, California, for example, once lost US$1.7 billion speculating on interest rate derivatives.

In Singapore, Nick Leeson is well known as the man who single-handedly broke Barings in 1995, having lost more than US$1.4 billion on derivatives positions. Sumitomo's chief copper trader lost US$3 billion for his company trading in derivatives in the mid 1990s.

Contemplating this scope for potential financial damage, it is no wonder that Warren Buffett has called derivatives "financial weapons of mass destruction".

IMPLICATIONS FOR YOU

There are a few basic observations for the potential retail investor in the world of options, derivatives and hedges:

- Have a clear use for each derivative investment.
- Stay away from anything you do not understand completely.
- Use these products only with a full awareness of the losses they can create.
- Take professional advice before entering this volatile arena.

❧ 31 ❧

PLANNING FOR THE
UNEXPECTED

Life does not always work out the way we hope or the way we plan. Perfect foresight, for better or worse, is not part of the human condition.

Although we cannot know and therefore cannot plan for everything that may lie ahead of us, we can take steps to prepare ourselves for the unexpected to some extent. The cause and nature of an emergency or major negative event may not be foreseeable, but the impact this event *might* have on our plans can be estimated through an intelligent awareness of the most likely possibilities and the potential consequences.

Having a carefully thought-through contingency plan in place can have a major positive impact on the creation and preservation of your wealth.

DYNAMIC ENVIRONMENT

We live in a dynamic universe. Change swirls around every aspect of our lives in patterns both visible and invisible.

According to chaos theory, one small change in a remote area of the world can lead to great disasters on the other side of the planet. The interconnected nature of all things will create unexpected changes in the shape of our lives. Being ready for these unexpected events can reduce both financial and emotional impact when and if they occur. As a result, every strategy needs a Plan B — including your financial strategy.

CATEGORIES OF RISK EVENTS

Very crudely, there are four categories of risk events which require thinking through in order to protect your finances.

By reviewing the most likely emergencies which could arise within each category of risk, you will be able to decide what action, if any, you can take in advance to prepare yourself to respond appropriately.

First, let us turn to the risks and then review the tools we can use to respond to them.

Full impact events: Unfortunately, there will always be major disasters which can affect everyone in a society, no matter how rich or poor, and over which we have no control. SARS, bird flu, flooding, tsunami, earthquakes and other terrible events can have an enormous impact on all aspects of our lives, including our financial plans — income, expenses, value of investments and other elements.

Income impact events: The impact of this second class of events will focus primarily on the income we receive. The greatest of these income impact events is the loss of employment. Employer bankruptcy, merger leading to job loss, downsizing, disagreements at work leading to dismissal and other unexpected situations can lead to the abrupt termination of your main, and possibly only, source of income. Another disastrous situation would be the permanent disability of a main breadwinner, again resulting in an inability to generate income.

Cost impact events: Cost impact events are those which could have a major impact on one or more of the elements of expense in our plan: A house may need extensive repair, a member of the family may fall ill and need extended or even permanent care, divorce, death or even unexpected births within the family can all have significant and unexpected cost impact.

Wealth impact events: In addition to events affecting our personal income and expense plans, external events can have a major impact on the value of our assets and future income potential. Stock markets go down as well as up. Businesses can fail. Property values can plunge if interest rates rise or tax policies change.

The list of possibilities within each category is endless, but with thought, discussion and insight you will perhaps be able to narrow it down to a few that could be more likely than others and are worth considering as you establish your Wealth Wisdom Plan.

After establishing the potential risk events for which you would like to be prepared, assess the impact of these events against the figures you have entered on your Annual Budget, Monthly Budget Tracker and Personal Wealth Schedule forms so that you can prepare your response.

PREPARE YOUR RESPONSE

Although we are unlikely to be capable of eliminating natural disasters or halting the spread of avian flu, we can address the trigger points of the more personal risks in advance:

- *Insurance:* Across all categories, insurance is the traditional risk management tool.
- *Contingency fund:* Some experts advise that we set aside savings which will cover three to six months of your outgoings in case of an emergency.
- *Balanced portfolio:* The specific risks to any single asset class highlight the value of a balanced approach to your savings and investments. Liquidity needs (the need to access cash on short notice,) may also change in a tough moment or crisis. The overall approach to asset allocation has already been discussed in Chapter 18, but should be reviewed again in the context of potential disasters and other emergency needs.
- *Conservative approach:* A more conservative asset allocation approach can also reduce risk.
- *Fast response:* In any difficult situation, the ability to act swiftly to limit the damage and correct a situation as quickly as possible has enormous value.

One of the reasons to work with high-quality professional advisers and to keep an eye on your investments yourself is to be able to spot problems early and respond as quickly as possible before the situation gets out of hand.

DARWINIAN WISDOM

In his book *On the Evolution of Species,* Charles Darwin did not use the phrase "survival of the fittest" or "only the strong survive". These words were written by others who were attempting to summarise his thoughts.

What Darwin actually said was that the species which adapted most quickly to changes in their environment were more likely to survive.

The same principle can apply when managing your own financial affairs. By planning, but also by being prepared to adapt to changes in your environment, you will be far more likely to ensure the survival of your wealth beyond the impact of the unexpected.

 భ 32 ళ

MAKING IT WORK FOR YOU

You have now finished Part III of *Wealth Wisdom for Everyone* and should be ready to complete Form III at the back of this book: Your Personal Wealth Schedule, the final part of your overall Wealth Wisdom Plan.

Wealth objectives and asset allocation: Before starting to enter your data in the Personal Wealth Schedule, it may be useful to have a quick review of Chapters 2, 3 and 18 addressing your wealth check, your wealth objectives and the asset allocation model.

Before setting out your target savings and investment sums, it is essential to know why you are making these investments from a top-down view. The questions in these chapters can help you to define what you are trying to accomplish. You may want to revisit the basic questions one more time:

- Do you want to generate income or capital gain, or both?
- Do you want low, medium or high risk?

- Will you want to access your cash quickly?
- Are there any life stage changes you want to prepare for?
- How much contingency funding do you need?
- Do you have adequate savings?
- Have you consulted a qualified financial adviser?

It is so important that your allocation of savings and investments matches your portfolio and specific objectives that they have all been included on Form III. By putting these three items together, you will be able to see how all three work together on one page.

You can complete your plan manually, using the paper forms attached here or you may wish to use the on-line versions available on the Channel NewsAsia website.

If you are using the paper forms, you may find it useful for future budget planning purposes, to make photocopies before you begin.

COMPLETING THE PERSONAL WEALTH SCHEDULE

1. Collect and prepare the documents and files for the current year as described in Chapter 4.
2. Confirm the data on your personal profile and review the implications.
3. List your highest priority wealth objectives in order next to the numbers 1, 2 and 3.
4. Think through the implications for your actual allocation of funds.
5. Decide upon the best mix for you (given your profile and objectives) of the categories in the table.
6. Enter the value of your property and any mortgage payment you might have associated with this property. The property value minus the mortgage gives you your Net Property Value.

7. Next, fill in the relevant numbers in the respective boxes for the individual categories.

Again, do not try to rush. You may want to reconsider how much to allocate to asset classes in which you do not yet have any exposure. You might want to keep some boxes empty if you feel that these asset categories are too risky.

8. If you have any other loans and debts, do not forget to take these into account and enter them in the appropriate box.

9. Adding up your Net Property Value and Total Savings and Investment figures and deducting any non-mortgage debts you might have, will determine your Personal Wealth:

Personal Wealth = Net Property Value plus Total Savings and Investments minus Total Non-Mortgage Debts.

10. As a final check, review all the numbers from an overall perspective. Do they look right? Have you forgotten anything? Your review should rely on your judgement as much as your number skills.

11. After completing Form III, it is still important to speak with a financial adviser before making an investment decision. The Personal Wealth Schedule should help to clarify your thinking and objectives — a very useful start to a conversation with a financial adviser.

USING THE ON-LINE FORMS

If you are using the on-line version of the forms, there are only a few differences in the process.

The on-line version can be used as follows:

1. Download the templates from the website.
2. Remember to save updated versions of the file as you go along.

3. The on-line form will automatically calculate your funds available for savings and investment.

Asset Allocation Review

As mentioned before, the ultimate objective of these planning and tracking exercises is to enable you to gain full control over your finances and to realise the full potential of your wealth creation capability. After filling out Form III, you may want to step back and compare it with your views on asset allocation developed in Chapter 18 and listed at the beginning of this chapter.

- Does your portfolio look too risky?
- Is it liquid enough, i.e. can you get cash out of it if you need to?
- Is the currency exposure right?
- Are the returns high enough to meet your objectives?
- Do you understand every category and product you have selected?
- Do you need to save or invest more of your income?
- Do you have the best advisers available?

And, of course:

- What does your professional adviser think of your proposal?

Part IV

LIFE CHANGES

❧ 33 ❧

MARRIAGE AND DIVORCE

Psychologists tell us that the three most stressful events in our lives are change of job, change of residence, and change of marital status. Although they may well be positive rather than negative events, each of them sets into motion a wave of change across many elements of our lives, including our financial plans.

Each of these three events, in addition to triggering strong emotions and changes in long established life patterns, signals the need for a fundamental review of virtually every aspect of our personal financial plans and approach to wealth management.

From basic objectives to the details of household expenses and insurance, each of these events creates the need for a complete rethink of your financial plans and, very likely, a whole new approach to managing your personal finances.

In this chapter we are focusing on the third of these 'high-stress' life events: Change of marital status and also additions to the family.

Within this one category there can be four significant status shifts. Each one is so significant in emotional and financial terms that it could be termed a paradigm change — one resulting in a whole new way of life.

These paradigm changes are marriage, the arrival of children, divorce and widowhood.

PARADIGM CHANGE I: MARRIAGE

Getting married, one of the most significant and beautiful moments of our lives, also has a seismic effect on finances, and not just those of the couple getting married. The effects may be felt equally by their parents. This is especially true if each member of the new couple has lived at home until marriage.

In this instance the changes in responsibilities and the financial consequences of the new-found status of all parties involved will be enormous.

For the newlyweds, a well-planned financial transition will help to reduce the shock of their new economic independence and responsibility. The couple's parents, on the other hand, may find themselves benefiting from a decrease in expenses and greater savings potential now that they have reduced their financial family responsibilities.

Two levels of plan adjustment

The financial impact of marriage is usually felt at two levels and therefore plans need to be adapted accordingly.

First are the one-off expenses directly related to the wedding and post-wedding arrangements: the cost of the ceremony itself, wedding outfits, gifts, honeymoon and perhaps the purchase and fitting out of a new home.

In some cases, generous parents and family might absorb some or even all of the event costs, but in others they may be shouldered by the bride and groom themselves. Every culture has a different approach to the responsibilities for marriage expenses and these should be reflected in the financial plans of all concerned, usually long before the event itself.

In addition to budgeting for one-off costs, annual income, expenditure, savings and investment targets will also need to be reset as it is very likely that almost every aspect of your previous plan will now have changed. Available income may increase if the newlyweds are both working. Taxes will need to be recalculated.

Not just income and expense

It is not just income and expense figures that will need to change on your financial plan for married life. Beneficiaries of insurance policies, healthcare coverage, car insurance policies and a whole host of other documentation may need to be changed. Mortgage responsibilities, debt obligations, educational plans and other items of great importance may also need to be revisited.

This can also be an excellent opportunity not just to transfer ownership of old assets or policies but to shop around for more cost-effective deals. In every great change there is always opportunity for improvement.

If both halves of the newly married couple already have financial plans, consolidation of the two will hopefully be a positive, rewarding and even fun exercise. On the other hand, if neither already has a plan, this provides a good opportunity to work together to prepare for a shared future.

PARADIGM CHANGE II: CHILDREN

The arrival of children in our lives is often an even bigger change than marriage. As well as giving us great pleasure, children can also give us financial headaches if the full impact of their arrival is not properly anticipated and built into a detailed financial plan.

As is the case for marriage, new, one-off and recurring expenses will need to be budgeted for, such as hospital fees, doctors' bills, house preparation, and other child-related items. There will also be significant changes made to long-term financial plans to provide care and protection for your new arrival. Education can be expensive and it makes sense to start saving as early as possible for your children's future.

The scale and nature of change is especially great with the birth of a first child. From personal and financial perspectives, you are moving into unknown territory. As such, it is doubly important for the parents-to-be to spend time planning in advance of the child's arrival, perhaps helped along with some wise advice from your own parents, or friends who already have children.

Investing the time up front to be as prepared as possible can ensure that you won't be coping with a double dose of stress as you face this new challenge.

PARADIGM CHANGE III: DIVORCE

Divorce is never easy and there are no winners when a family breaks up.

Although a sad way to benefit from your earlier efforts, the existence of a clearly documented financial plan will make the divorce process less painful. Records will be easily at hand, asset and liability (debt) registers up to date, bank statements available and household costs defined. All of these early efforts to run a unified home in a responsible and far-sighted way will help in the unfortunate event of divorce.

As for marriage and the birth of a child, your financial plan will need to be reassessed. Again, a combination of one-off costs and on-going expenses will need to be considered. Two separate plans will need to be drafted where before only one was needed.

One-off costs will include legal fees and the expenses involved in setting up a second home, both of which can add up to a significant sum. These one-off costs can wipe out projected savings and investment contributions for many years to come.

Annual income and expenditure figures will also need to be revised. Alimony, maintenance, travel to and from different residences, long-distance telephone charges, separate vacation expenses and other recurring costs need to be assessed and built into new financial plans for life after separation and divorce.

Avoid litigation if at all possible

In order to emerge from divorce proceedings with your wealth intact — even if it is divided into two separate holdings — all legal experts recommend that the couple divorcing avoid litigation if at all possible.

Lawyers' fees can mount up very quickly; enormous amounts of time and money are wasted, job performances suffer, income is lost, children are damaged and friendships lost as those close to the feuding couple are dragged into the fray.

In one court case, a millionaire and his wife in Hong Kong were locked in such an obsessive battle of uncontrolled egos and fruitless revenge that they lost all of the money they had carefully accumulated together over the course of a quarter of a century. Instead of amicably settling their differences and going their separate ways, they both destroyed their happy memories and wasted all their hard-earned wealth on lawyers' fees.

This stands as a great example of how *not* to manage a life transition.

The parenting angle

You never stop being a parent, no matter how old your offspring. Parenting is a lifelong pleasure and obligation, taking many forms over the years. Being there as a caring and responsible source of strength in trying family times is one of the most valuable, even if one of the most difficult, burdens we shoulder.

It is possible, in some circumstances, that the parents of a divorced couple may also need to readjust their budget to take into account the additional costs of assuming their old responsibilities once again, should their child need to move back home or their grandchildren need support.

PARADIGM CHANGE IV: WIDOWHOOD

It is a sad statistical reality that many wives outlive their husbands. After the death of a husband, a widow may not have been fully prepared on a financial basis for this stage of life. Widowhood may not bring with it a regular flow of income, healthcare coverage or pension benefits.

In the past, the extended family cared for, and perhaps even revolved around, the matriarch in some cultures. In modern times, this traditional structure may have been left behind and inadequate attention paid to a widow's needs in an expensive modern world.

It is important to review all insurance and pension documents, as well as ownership of important assets, to ensure that either half of a couple will be well taken care of once the other dies.

If appropriate, it could be a useful exercise to review a financial plan from a widow's perspective, analysing income expenses and assets with a view to living for an extended number of years without a spouse.

∞ 34 ∞

CHILDREN AND
MULTI-GENERATIONAL FAMILIES

Attitudes to the important subjects of children and multi-generational families vary enormously from family to family and from culture to culture.

In many Asian families, it is still traditional for grandparents, parents and children to live under the same roof, dining, working and socialising together. In other cultures, children leave home when they go to university and return, from then on, only for vacations or visits. This more independent pattern is typical of many Western families — Scandinavian, American and other Anglo-Saxon nationalities in particular.

There is no 'right' way for families to live, but what *is* necessary is to have a clear understanding of your own family model and the implications of that model on all aspects of the planning and management of family affairs.

The role of children within the family also varies enormously between cultures. In some, the age of childhood is a relatively recent concept. For example, children in some countries in Western Europe in past centuries were considered merely as young adults. This attitude is illustrated in historical paintings where children are dressed in miniature versions of adults' clothing and have faces that often seem old far beyond their years.

Even today some children are brought up to be involved in business affairs from a very early age, taking on chores and even attending the board meetings of companies they are to inherit.

In other instances, children are left to enjoy their childhood with little discipline or engagement in the more serious world of adult affairs. There is seen to be plenty of time to teach societal and commercial values to children who might shy away from such responsibilities at so tender an age.

Although these two subjects are related in that they both reflect the level of responsibility given to children at different ages, let us take up the issues of multi-generational families and the role of children within the family separately.

CHILDREN

Children, according to leading psychologists, need two things from their parents in order to be happy: love and discipline. Children want to learn about life, to prepare for the challenges they will face and to be able to pursue their dreams secure in the knowledge that they are loved, and also with the valuable understanding of where their boundaries lie.

Involvement in budgeting

Responsible families will make the effort to involve their children in selected aspects of their budgeting and wealth planning at an early age. They believe children should learn the value of things, that money is not infinite and that an open discussion can help to prepare children for greater financial challenges later on.

While not appropriate to discuss all aspects of family finances with children who have yet to learn the value of discretion, selective involvement in certain areas can teach children about the costs borne by their parents for education, sports and other out-of-school activities, entertainment, holidays and even how much it costs to feed and clothe a family.

Basic financial learning

It may be beneficial for children to be exposed to some of the basic disciplines of income and expenditure from an early age. Some of these activities have provided a good starting point for children across all cultural barriers.

Chores: To learn the basics about income, children can be given a set of chores that must be performed on a daily or weekly basis in return for a small financial reward or a regular allowance. Tidying a bedroom is perhaps not enough. Other small jobs such as feeding pets, washing dishes or watering plants can all be good lessons on how to contribute towards family life.

Allowance: In many families, children will receive a regular allowance. The amount will vary according to the age of the child, the family's means and, possibly, the chores that have been set. Children's allowances can be the subject of much lively family discussion once the topic is raised and ideas invited from all concerned.

Some families have adopted an ingenious allowance system which achieves many objectives simultaneously. In this system, children are given an amount equal to their age; a 6-year-old gets six dollars per week and a 12-year-old gets twelve dollars and so on. The allowance is then divided into three equal portions. One third is allocated to savings, a second third to a charity of the child's choice and another third to spending. This first portion can be kept as cash in a strongbox at home so children can see their money 'grow' and learn the value of saving.

The value of giving can be learned by giving the second portion to a deserving charity. As mentioned above, the final third is allocated for spending, either on a weekly basis or saved up for a special, perhaps more expensive, purchase.

This approach can be a valuable step toward learning the value of financial responsibility and the pursuit of various objectives.

Accounts: From the age of six or seven onward, when children can add and subtract, some families ask their children to keep a small account book to record their own income (i.e. allowance) expenditures and cash on hand. Allowances are only paid upon the demonstration of up-to-date accounts and the completion of chores.

Setting an example

Although, as we have already mentioned, children should not be exposed to the more sensitive elements of family finances until they are old enough to understand and be discreet about such information, it is a good idea to talk to them about the tasks required and the benefits that can be gained from sound financial planning.

With this understanding and your good example, your children are far more likely to grow up to be financially responsible.

Children and their parents can also access a number of websites which will help them deal with money matters. Many young children are now more adept at using online resources than their parents these days, and working direct with them to find and discuss interesting information sources may be an opportunity to learn together.

MULTI-GENERATIONAL FAMILIES

Although multi-generational households are still common, particularly among Asian families, it is not perhaps as easy as it used to be to keep such households together. In particular, many members of the younger generation are adopting a more independent, Western model of behaviour. This makes it all the more important to be specific about what is expected of each individual and of the family in return.

What financial rights and obligations does each member of a multi-generational household have? How will these obligations be affected with changes in family dynamics?

Income and expenditure

There are obvious implications for all aspects of an income and expenditure plan for a multi-generational family. Income may or may not be higher in the context of a larger family unit, but costs will almost certainly be greater than those of a smaller family, while housing will probably be less costly than when living in separate residences. Medical cover, insurance, transport, school fees and other costs will all have to be tailored to fit the extended family's needs.

Assets and liabilities

The same clarity will be required for family savings and investments. The ownership of assets, the nature of loans and decisions about how and where investments will be made can be a complex process in a household where everyone has a say. The issue of property rights can lead to disputes if not clarified and managed properly.

By finding new ways to accommodate old patterns, traditional values can be preserved for everyone concerned.

Business assets

One of the biggest issues facing multi-generational families is the management and disposition of family business assets. Ownership of the assets, control over a family business and related issues can tear apart even the closest of families. The psychology of a founding entrepreneur may make him feel more attached to his business than he is to his own children.

It is preferable that clarity on matters concerning family business ownership and control should not need to wait until the reading of a will.

Trusts and estate planning

Trusts allow assets to be protected from taxes, and are especially useful in jurisdictions with a disadvantageous inheritance tax regime.

Trusts allow a donor (the 'testator') to place his or her assets into a legal vehicle for a pre-set number of years or the length of a 'life in being' plus 21 years. A 'life in being' is the life of anyone you choose to name, including an infant, as long as they are alive at the time of the establishment of the trust.

A trust allows you, for example, to tie up your property assets for the life of your child plus a period in which his son or daughter might be too young to make responsible decisions. In this case, the assets will be managed by a nominated trustee in accordance with the terms set out in the trust documents.

Trusts, once described by an Oxford law professor as 'distrusts' — an invention for fathers who didn't trust their sons — can be an effective way to distribute assets within a family structure after an original wealth creator has died.

Insurance beneficiaries

Some of the same complexity arises with regard to substantial life insurance payments. Who will receive what from whom at which time and for which reason? The number of potential answers to these questions is enormous, signalling the need for clear financial planning in an area where clarity may not always be easy to achieve in a multi-generational family context.

HAPPY FAMILIES

Oscar Wilde once said that happy families were boring because they were all the same. Unhappy families, he wrote, were far more interesting because they were all so different in their dysfunctionality.

While a financial plan is no guarantee for happiness, a team effort to understand and share in the realisation of a family wealth plan may help to build a sense of shared responsibility and accomplishment in your own family.

☙ 35 ☙

WEALTH AND HEALTH

It is no coincidence that the first of these three famous aspirations — healthy, wealthy and wise — deals with our physical
and mental well-being.

If we suffer from serious health problems, it is difficult to
maximise income, manage expenses and invest sufficiently to
achieve ambitious wealth creation objectives. Major illnesses
and accidents, even when we are fully insured, will inevitably
have a significant negative effect on family economics as well
as on practical, emotional and other important aspects of family life.

Addressing the financial impact of the vast range of
health issues facing us today would require the luxury of far
more time and space than we have available in this one chapter. We would like instead to offer a few suggestions for
planning and, where possible, preventative actions that you
can take to help minimise the impact that ill health can have
on your Wealth Wisdom Plan.

In so doing, we must consider the implications both of a health crisis (illness or accident) and of living a healthy lifestyle. Each of these can have a major impact on our financial as well as our physical and mental health.

PREVENTION AND CURE

It has long been said that an ounce of prevention is worth a pound of cure. In the case of a Wealth Wisdom Plan, a few cents spent on prevention may save you many dollars spent on a cure. It is far more sensible to invest in staying healthy than to face the chronic costs of ill health.

HEALTH CRISES

Sudden illness, accident, incapacitation or disability can invalidate any existing personal wealth plan. It is very likely that income will decrease, possibly even stop altogether. Costs will almost certainly increase and savings may need to be withdrawn to pay for medical bills and care.

Experts estimate now that 90% of the medical expenses in our lifetimes are incurred in the last 10 days of our lives. None of us wants our spouses or children to have to shoulder the final costs of our own mortality or extended infirmity.

Careful forward planning can help us cope with these unexpected health crises. Chapter 10: Insurance, explains how you can set plans in place to prevent potential health issues from becoming financial disasters. The health risks to insure against vary by country and racial group. In India, diabetes is a major issue, in China, pulmonary diseases are prevalent and in Japan, liver cancer is a disproportionate risk.

It is useful to review all elements of your plan with a good financial adviser who can help you to understand the full impact a medical crisis would have on your finances. *In particular, you may want to ask him to what extent you might be exposed to costs not covered by insurance.*

CHRONIC HEALTH ISSUES

If we suffer from a chronic illness such as asthma, diabetes, low blood pressure, migraine headaches, food allergies or other long-term ailment, this will also have an impact on our income and expenditure.

It is possible that our income will be affected as we may need to take more time off work than normal (or allowable), but we are also likely to bear extra medical expenses and these, unlike the insurable risks mentioned above, may not be covered by insurance.

LIFESTYLE DISEASES

Ironically, as our medical expertise grows and we find more and more effective responses to heart attacks, cancers and other diseases, our lifestyle choices are creating even larger problems for our societies.

Smoking, unhealthy diets, obesity, excessive alcohol consumption and other lifestyle ailments have a massive impact on national economies. If we are not careful, they can have an equally massive impact on our own lives and individual financial plans. This is where preventative action can be taken to minimise negative financial consequence.

Take smoking as an example. In Singapore, a packet of 20 cigarettes now costs around S$12. One pack a day thus costs

S$4,380 per year of after-tax income. So, the amount of after-tax income required to fund a 40-year smoking habit will total S$175,200. To this already large sum should be added the extra cost of insurance since smokers pay higher premiums than non-smokers. Lost income, due to a higher incidence of health problems and a shorter life expectancy, should also be factored into your plans.

While this is not intended to be a lecture on how to lead a perfect life, it is perhaps worth stopping for a moment to consider how much could have been 'harvested' from the investment of this substantial sum instead of it literally going up in smoke.

VIRTUES AND VALUES

Wealth Wisdom provides a balanced and complete approach to the management of your financial affairs. A similar approach might be useful in the physical and mental health spheres as well. Healthy eating, regular exercise, meditation, moderation in drinking and abstaining from smoking can have a substantially positive impact on your financial plans as well as on your physical or family life.

Moderation in all things may be a short statement that has a long and positive impact on many aspects of our lives.

WISDOM BEYOND WEALTH

Investing in your health through regular check-ups, a balanced lifestyle and a full programme of healthy habits can give you the best possible quality of life and, at the same time, reduce the amount of money spent on medical costs which could otherwise be working hard for you in a savings or investment plan.

This investment in your physical well-being may be one of the best investments you can make for the financial and emotional health of you and your family.

⤚ 36 ⤙

RETIREMENT

There are three key aspects of retirement which need to be considered in order to prepare your Wealth Wisdom Plan. Each aspect is strongly interrelated and each requires a decision which can have a profound impact on the content of your plan from beginning to end. These three aspects are:

- Your retirement age.
- Your retirement lifestyle.
- Your retirement funding.

DETERMINING YOUR RETIREMENT AGE

In every thoughtful financial plan, it is of critical importance to determine at which age you plan to retire. Are you planning to retire at the age of 65 as many Americans do, at 55 as many Asians do, or at 35 as a very few entrepreneurs and sports figures do? Or are you one of the driven few who look forward to working until you are 90 years old or beyond?

Sumner Redstone, a famous American billionaire born in 1923 and still running his media empire more than eighty years later, jokingly informed the public recently that he is having so much fun he is actively trying to figure out how to take his business with him when he goes.

Most companies offer a more ordinary range of retirement options with different associated benefits. These options need to be fully understood and their consequences tested by developing different retirement model variations on your basic plan.

Establishing your retirement age will determine when income generation will stop, or at least be substantially reduced. A decision to take early retirement may buy you more leisure time, but can lop off many high-income-earning years from your career, reduce monthly retirement benefits and require you to eat into savings and investments at an earlier date than anticipated. Deferred retirement can have an opposite – and often highly positive – impact on the quality of your later years.

Minister Mentor Lee Kwan Yew in Singapore, Queen Elizabeth II of England, as well as former US President Ronald Reagan, management guru Peter Drucker and Linus Pauling (these last two both worked until they were over 90 years old) all demonstrate that life does not need to end upon arrival at a predetermined retirement age.

Your retirement age, together with the level of income you would like to enjoy through your retirement, will determine the amount of money you need to set aside during your working life.

Starting to save early and managing your wealth carefully are virtues that will lead to truly golden years after the end of your working life.

DEFINING YOUR RETIREMENT LIFESTYLE

How you plan to live after the day of your retirement will also have a critical impact on the amount of capital and future income you will need to have ready on the day you retire. The range of expense patterns is enormous and will depend upon your personal choices and personal means. The needs vary dramatically between a retired life spent at home watching television, with the lights extinguished to preserve electricity, and a life spent jetting around the world drinking champagne and buying precious works of art.

Most of us are likely to seek some pathway between these two extremes, but in order to achieve our expectations, whatever they may be, we must be able to anticipate and plan for the cost of our desired retirement lifestyle.

Travel, entertainment, gifts, educational support for grandchildren, healthcare, housing and a whole host of other items may change as you age. With extended expectations of life and increases in healthcare costs, the amounts necessary to live the way we want to live throughout our retirements are going up all the time.

All elements of your wealth plan should be looked at from a retirement angle long before you near retirement age. For example, a mortgage fully paid-off before retirement can remove many concerns. Alternatively, the purchase of a multi-generational house, providing family support and cost-sharing possibilities as well as physical shelter may be an insightful decision you can make well before your retirement.

Neither should we forget to allow for the risk of inflation. Living on a fixed pension (one with no cost of living adjustment, or 'COLA') can be difficult when living expenses are increasing steadily over the years.

When looking at way to reduce your costs in retirement, you should also make sure you take full advantage of all the benefits of senior citizenship open to you. These may include special rate (or even free) memberships, municipal services, travel and many other areas of expense.

FUNDING YOUR RETIREMENT

The final aspect to consider when formulating your wealth plan for retirement is how you will fund your retirement years.

While the income component of your financial plan may be relatively straightforward while you are working, during your retirement years the number of income sources, and the level of each, may create a more complex income model.

Your retirement income could be funded from a wide range of sources. Many of these sources have already been discussed in detail in previous chapters of this book, but in summary:

Public and private pensions: You should take a hard look at the realistic annual income you can expect from a public or private pension scheme and decide — if permitted within a public scheme — whether your pension contributions could be better invested elsewhere. See Chapter 25: Pensions, for more information.

Savings: Savings need to be carefully managed. Interest rates can go down as well as up. Careful attention to obtaining the maximum return by longer term instruments and shopping for the best rates is necessary.

Investments: The optimal level and mix of investments — equities, bonds, property and other — for your personal situation will need to be determined for your unique personal situation. One old formula stipulates that the percentage of equities in your portfolio should be one hundred, minus your age. Although too crude in a multi-asset class world, this old rule of thumb does underscore the importance of a shift to less high-risk and more income generating investments as we become older.

Investments in retirement: Active investing, with appropriate risk parameters, can generate income to support or enhance a retirement lifestyle. There is no need to freeze a portfolio at age 55 or 65; active participation in various investments such as property development and portfolio management can go on long after we stop going to the office from nine to five every day.

Annuities: Annuities are financial instruments purchased in one go or funded over time which yield a fixed income from a set date until the end of a life. These products are available from many providers and should be reviewed in the context of your specific goals for an overall savings, investment and insurance plan.

Advanced insurance payout: Some insurance policies have an option to pay out in either a lump sum or in an annuity form before death. You should understand the full benefits and costs of such an approach in the context of your overall life insurance and retirement income objectives. See Chapter: 10 Insurance, for more information.

Property income: Property can be a valuable source of capital appreciation (in the right market), can play a role as a hedge against inflation and can also provide income for a full lifetime. Although rental yields (the ratio of rental income from a property compared to — and expressed as a percentage of — its capital value) may be relatively low in some countries, the multiple roles played by property may make it an attractive element in many retirement income strategies. See Chapter 19: Property, for more information.

Reverse mortgage: Another possibility for the generation of additional income from property during retirement is to take out a reverse mortgage. In a reverse mortgage, you get a lump sum, loan line or a series of regular payments from a bank, which builds up a financial obligation for your estate.

As a result, you have funds available during your lifetime but a potentially large debt to be paid later. Chapter 11: Mortgages explains how a reverse mortgage works in more detail.

Family support: In many cultures, for a very long time, a reliable model of retirement has included family support in old age. In some countries, such as Singapore, parents even have a legal right to be supported financially by their children.

Having supported and financed children through their early years, parents could expect to receive a 'pay back' by way of support from their children in later years. This expectation may need to be clarified and reviewed in today's world, where social mobility, cross-cultural marriages and international careers can disturb established patterns even if good intentions are present in the younger generation.

Another issue to keep in mind is that this model worked well when families were larger and the care of parents could be shared among many. But with smaller families, who in turn have even smaller families, this system may no longer work the way it used to. In addition, more women (the traditional caregivers and homemakers) are often now working and cannot take on the roles they played in the past.

Active earnings: It is not only the high and mighty who can work profitably into their later years. Second careers, part-time work and even entrepreneurial start-ups can provide a fresh source of income and wealth creation during an active 'retirement' phase.

PLANNING FOR THE UNEXPECTED

Retirement planning, like all other areas of financial planning, must allow for some element of the unexpected. Protracted illness, an accident, the need for extra domestic help, major car repairs, emergency financial assistance for children or grandchildren and other unexpected calamities can all throw off even the most thoroughly thought-through retirement plans.

The early setting aside of a contingency sum for retirement can add both an extra financial buffer and extra peace of mind at a time when unexpected demands and unpleasant surprises can be particularly disturbing.

∾ 37 ∾

ESTATE PLANNING

Estate planning is more than just having a will.

A will is the centrepiece of an effective estate plan but other financial aspects also need to be taken into account. These include estate liquidity, having enough cash in easily accessed accounts to pay for probate costs, funeral expenses, estate duties and other estate-related expenses.

The use of life insurance proceeds, the transfer of assets (with special thought being given to shares of jointly owned assets) and being able to access all necessary documents, secure storage and safety deposit boxes also need to be taken into consideration.

Some people avoid discussing death out of a superstitious fear of attracting ill winds or hastening a death which we think, at some level, is a fate we may be able to avoid. When it comes to financial planning, this superstitious attitude can be very expensive indeed.

There are perhaps three key certainties about death which will have an impact on our financial plans. First, death will come to all of us. Second, it is unlikely that our death will come at a time of our choosing. And finally, our death will affect those left behind far more than it will affect us.

Two great writers confirm these certainties and remind us, with wise words from the past, of truths we should heed when facing our present responsibilities.

William Shakespeare confirmed the first two certainties mentioned above when he wrote, in *Julius Caesar*:

"It seems to me most strange that men should fear;
Seeing that death, a necessary end,
Will come when it will come".

These words are extremely important as we face the issue of death as an integral part of our financial planning. Death does not often arrive according to our schedule and so it is essential that we prepare a plan for our death and are ready to execute that plan at any time.

A second great author, Thomas Mann, writing in *The Magic Mountain*, offered a wise view of death which is very instructive for those who desire to preserve wealth and to influence other lives after the "necessary end" of their own. He wrote:

"A man's dying is more the survivors' affair than his own."

If we do not face our responsibilities properly before we die, we will only make life more difficult for those we love and leave behind; those who will already be struggling with the spiritual and emotional stress of our departing.

WEALTH PRESERVATION

Having worked for an entire lifetime to build up and preserve our wealth, the last thing any of us would like to see is a great part of that financial estate inadvertently left to people we did not intend to benefit from our efforts or, even worse, to the tax authorities.

Preparing in advance to streamline our affairs from a tax perspective, especially in a country with high levels of estate duties, can also ensure that our beneficiaries receive the largest possible share of the wealth we intend to leave for them.

ESTATE DUTIES

The amount of inheritance tax taken by the government varies enormously from country to country and even from one time period to another within the same country. Rates can vary from zero to more than 50%. In order to plan effectively, it is important to know which country will claim a share of your assets, what the prevailing rates are and how they apply to your own situation.

In some countries, wives pay nothing on the estate they inherit from their husbands. The children of the deceased may pay lower rates than cousins, nephews, nieces or other relatives who share in the inheritance. Friends, charities and other non-related parties may have to pay a much higher rate on their inheritance.

PLAN AND ACT EARLY

It is worth giving serious consideration to the opportunities which can be taken to reduce estate duty. In some countries, trusts and settlements that are in place five years or more before death are not taxed as a death duty item. This would argue for an earlier start to estate planning than we might ordinarily consider.

A second approach is to look at your tax code's application to different types of assets. If a primary residence is passed on tax-free and cash or financial assets attract duty in the country where your estate will be taxed, it may be wise to invest in an expensive home and use up much of your cash in the purchase to avoid paying unnecessary taxes.

By starting to plan early for estate duties and future wealth distribution, we may find a few small actions today that can keep our estates from paying a significant amount of tax in the future.

GET ORGANISED

In every country, there is a prescribed legal process to follow when someone dies which requires a statement of assets and liabilities to be assembled, documents to be submitted and reports to be filed. This process, called probate in many English-speaking countries, ensures that all rules are observed, all debts and taxes paid in the correct order and that all local laws have been followed with regard to the winding up of the economic affairs of an individual's life.

To help those left behind with this process, one should ensure that all of the relevant documents are in one place. Bank statements, property deeds, mortgage documents, life insurance documents, birth certificates, business records, share certificates, credit card statements, tax filings and all other documents of importance can be easily processed if neatly assembled, organised and filed in one location.

These documents should be kept in a safe place. A fire-proof filing box may be sufficient for most of us. This box, it should be remembered, should be kept in a place known to more than just ourselves.

Where There is a Will There is a Way

Of these documents, one of the most important is your will. Every adult should have a will.

If you do not have a current will with which you are entirely satisfied, you should not hesitate to see a professional adviser to get one drafted, signed and witnessed.

Failing to draft and execute a will can lead to distribution of your worldly goods in a manner you would not have selected yourself, payment of unnecessary taxes and hurt feelings on the part of those inadvertently left out by your lack of effort.

There are three common reasons that people give for failing to make a will:

- I am too young to need a will.
- I didn't get around to doing it.
- I find it depressing to think about dying.

In all three cases it is clear that there is only minimal effort required to start — and finish — the process.

Where there is a will there is indeed a way.

Content of a Will

The purpose of a will is to transfer your worldly goods, after your death, in a manner which is both efficient and effective.

By *efficient* we mean transferring funds to the intended beneficiaries with as little cost to process the will (avoiding high commissions on the sale of property, unnecessary financial charges on account closure, avoidable lawyers' fees, etc) and as little tax payment as possible.

By *effective* we mean that the will should ensure that the wishes of the person whose estate is being transferred are fully respected in the final distribution of funds and properties.

A good will should ensure that the right beneficiaries get the largest sums possible in the manner and at the time you intend.

The required contents of a will vary from country to country, but the broad elements are often the same. These include:

- Name, address and other legal details (for example national identity card number).
- Name of the person or firm who will execute the will.
- List of assets and liabilities.
- List of beneficiaries and what value is to be given to each (financial and specific items).
- Names of your children's guardians (if children are still young at the time the will is drawn up or at the time of your death).
- Names and contact details of your advisers, including lawyer, tax accountant and any others who may make the probate process easier.

While the structure of the will is relatively standard, exact instructions can vary enormously. Some wills are very simple and leave everything to one person. Others may be very complicated and require assets to be distributed to many beneficiaries. Some may leave everything to a spouse and children while others may skip a generation entirely and leave everything to the grandchildren of the person making the will.

Some wills can reflect the unique personality, and even the whims, of the deceased. One famous writer recently left a specific sum of money for his friends to spend drinking to his memory at Harry's Bar in Venice.

Friends, pets, charities, churches, schools, favourite teachers and friendly local postmen have all found themselves included in wills. In some cases the inclusion was expected, in others the participation in the distribution of another person's assets may have come as a complete surprise.

MAKING A WILL

While there are various forms available in books and on the internet, it is highly recommended that you consult a lawyer or qualified accountant when making your will. He or she can describe the process required and the form recommended to ensure that your wishes are respected.

For example, it may be worthwhile to exclude individuals specifically from your estate or else you may leave the door open for future lawsuits by individuals who claim to have been accidentally left out of the will.

A professional can also give advice on how to structure the ownership of your assets and address all relevant personal and legal issues properly. It may be worthwhile for you to bring along your financial plan and index to the documents you have organised as described in Chapter 4 to help to describe what you have and what you intend to do with it.

IF NO WILL EXISTS

If no will exists, a person is said to have died 'intestate'. The treatment of the estate of persons who do not leave a 'testament' varies from country to country. In most countries there are prescribed distributions to wife and children which are followed through by a court-appointed executor. In addition, estate duties for individuals who die intestate in some countries are higher than they are for people who leave a will.

Another risk in not leaving a will is that the court will have to appoint someone to act as your executor. This may not be the person you would have chosen and they may not understand how you intended to leave your estate between the potential beneficiaries.

HANDWRITTEN WILLS

A handwritten will, also called a 'holographic will', can be valid without being witnessed in some countries. If you do not have a will in place, this could provide a quick stopgap measure while you draft something more permanent that may take some time to finalise.

As in all areas related to estate planning, before taking any action, check the laws of your own country to ensure your actions will have legal validity and that you are acting in the most appropriate manner to achieve your financial objectives in your estate distribution.

VARIATIONS ON THE THEME

When writing a will, many people only consider what happens if they die before those to whom they wish to leave their money. This may not be enough.

Sometimes children die before their parents, or younger siblings before their older brothers and sisters. Provision should also be made for the possibility of a husband and wife dying together.

It is never pleasant to think about these possibilities but, as the great writers quoted earlier in this chapter have stated far more eloquently than we, the time of any death is not of our choosing.

INCAPACITATION

With the advance of medical technology, it is possible that we could find ourselves incapacitated, mentally or physically, long before we die. The appropriate action to take in this unfortunate circumstance should also be considered.

REVISE WHEN NEEDED

Your will should be seen as a dynamic document. It should be amended as and when you experience a significant change in any aspect of your life which will affect the content of the will.

Extra assets or liabilities need to be taken into account. Births and deaths can change the beneficiaries and their intended allocations. Religious beliefs can change, as can the charities selected for consideration.

In the absence of any major life changes, your will should be reviewed at least once a year.

DISCUSS YOUR PLANS

Despite the great sensitivity of the topic, it is wise to discuss the terms of your will with a few trusted family members, friends and advisers. A combination of new ideas, valuable advice and technical detail can provide input to make your will operate after your death as you intended it to operate when you drafted it during your life.

WISDOM AS AN ADDITIONAL LEGACY

These days, some far-sighted individuals are also leaving 'ethical wills' for their beneficiaries through video, DVD or other formats.

These wills are not meant to change the formal distribution of financial assets, but are statements of belief, summaries of values, recounting of personal history and memories and explanations of important views or principles held by the grantor of the will.

It may be a sobering fact to remember that only one family in seven successfully preserves wealth beyond three generations. Those that do succeed are likely to have built their fortunes on a foundation of sustainable values.

Passing on those values can be a major gift to ensure that further generations benefit from your wisdom as well as your wealth.

Trusts

Trusts are legal vehicles which can be used in advance of a will being executed, or set up as part of the estate of an individual. A trust can accomplish many purposes; it can transfer money tax-effectively, distribute funds in the future based upon the specific wishes of an individual, delay transfer of funds and a whole host of other objectives. A typical trust with multiple objectives could, for example, transfer funds to an intended beneficiary only upon that person reaching the age of 21 and completing a degree from an accredited university.

Trust law will vary enormously from country to country, and even from religion to religion. Trusts and corporations can play a role in the estate plans of wealthy individuals and should be considered as part of your own plan upon the advice of a competent lawyer or tax expert from your own country.

'Heir Conditioning'

'Heir conditioning' is the amusing term used to describe the preparation of the inheritors of an estate, or of a business, to take up the responsibilities (and benefits) of the inheritance. Proper preparation will be pursued after the development of a specific plan set to reinforce the appropriate values and to teach the lessons needed in the most appropriate manner.

A well-thought-through preparation can include special schooling, a series of jobs to accumulate needed skills, separate discussions about responsibilities and expectations, the need to impart a balanced view of life (especially since it is never sure that today's assets will still be there tomorrow) and other non-financial understanding.

On the financial side, a phased approach to the transfer of assets and the establishment of trust funds (even small ones) can achieve specific goals in the process of preparation.

Too often, entrepreneurs, busy parents and heads of families do not pay enough attention to the moral and professional development of those who will inherit the assets developed by those who preceded them.

Far-sighted parents and testators will take an active and early interest in all aspects of 'conditioning' of the heirs to whom they plan to leave their worldly goods.

RELIGIOUS PRINCIPLES OF INHERITANCE

Some religions have specific requests and recommendations which may need to be taken into account when drafting a will. Some faiths recommend, or even require, that a set amount be allocated to charitable purposes. Others require all children to be treated equally.

Still others, for example the Islamic faith, have very specific doctrines designating specific roles and rights to individuals according to a formal system of relationship and tradition within a particular school of belief.

More than Just a Will

An estate plan, as we said at the beginning of this chapter, is more than just having a will.

A full estate plan aligns all aspects of your financial and personal affairs to achieve the objectives you set for your estate. By preparing fully in advance, you will be far more likely to ensure that your estate passes on as smoothly and efficiently as possible to those whom you wish to benefit from your own life's work and accumulated wisdom.

∞ 38 ∞

CONCLUSION

In the end is a beginning.

As for any strategic exercise — and Wealth Wisdom is all about providing a platform for your own wealth creation strategy — the approach you can undertake is both top-down and bottom-up.

The 'top-down' element is obtained through a high-level view of your finances and an approach which encompasses all assets and liabilities, all items of income and expense. The picture is complete and fully coordinated.

In addition, your Personal Wealth Schedule allows you to take a mountaintop view of your personal investment profile, wealth objectives and the resulting allocation of assets on one page. The portfolio of savings and investment products you select needs to be viewed as a set of separate parts and as an integrated portfolio where the whole should be worth more than the sum of the individual parts.

Wealth Wisdom is also built 'bottom-up', since it allows you to build a picture of your desired financial situation using all of the individual elements that make up your financial life. The approach taken ensures that all of your wealth creation objectives have been considered and the items in the templates, with supporting information, are complete, correct and fully understood in the context of an overall plan.

Although the templates are useful and your Wealth Wisdom Plans will provide you with an informed pathway forward, it is essential also to remember that any strategy or plan is only a means to a greater end.

In the introduction to *Wealth Wisdom for Everyone*, a number of questions were raised as challenges to your own state of readiness in the area of personal financial planning. As we reach the end of the book, it may be useful to revisit those early questions and review some of the content of the book to provide insights for your consideration:

- *Where can I best invest my money so it achieves the objectives I set for myself?*

  There is no ideal model for investment which works for everyone. Based on your age, wealth, life stage, financial sophistication, appetite for risk, need for income and other factors, you can set the best balance to achieve your objectives. By setting out a full and clear set of objectives, you will be able to define what your investment needs are and how to achieve them with available financial resources.

- *What are the biggest mistakes people usually make in investing? Why is that? How can I avoid their mistakes?*

  The biggest mistakes in investing arise from overconfidence. People don't cut their losses soon enough and believe they are better than they really are when it comes to financial management. You may be able to reduce the impact of overconfidence by, for example, setting stop-loss positions which trigger the sale of a share if it dips below a certain point.

- *How should we think about managing our careers? Is maximising next year's income the best way to build wealth? If not, what is the best approach to career management?*

Managing for lifetime income is far better than maximising next year's income. This may require a reduction in salary for a while — or even no salary at all if an educational degree is being pursued — in the pursuit of the larger goal of maximum lifetime income.

- *When should I start saving?*

The earlier the better. Compound interest rewards those who save early by adding interest on interest for a longer period of time. People who save early and save a substantial percentage of their income are far better off at retirement than their less responsible friends and colleagues.

- *Are there any practical ideas I can use to start teaching my children or grandchildren about financial responsibility? About social responsibility?*

Keeping simple accounts which require parental review before an allowance is paid, along with a set of regular chores, can be a valuable experience. One other initiative which teaches both forms of responsibility is an allowance which is divided up into thirds; one third each for saving, spending and charity.

- *What is the right level of expense?*

The right level of expense varies from individual to individual and from family to family, but one simple formula reverses the order of priorities and sets out a useful equation for your review: income minus savings equals expenses. This formula highlights the need to place a priority on savings rather than spending.

- *How much money should I save to achieve my financial objectives?*

This depends on you — your age, marital status, income expectations and retirement plans. Experts say a minimum of 10% is appropriate, with much higher levels necessary if you want to build your wealth more quickly.

- *Who should have a financial plan?*

Everyone should have a financial plan and most family members should participate in the process. Within the family, the most organised person may be the best one to do the planning and monitoring.

- *When do I need to redo my financial plan?*

You should redo your financial plan every year as a regular item on the calendar, but also when there is a big life change. Such changes could be a marriage, the birth of a child, a move to another house or country, a purchase of a residence, or any other change with a significant impact on income, expense, savings pattern or net worth.

- *Is having a will enough? Do I need to do more for estate planning?*

There is much more to estate planning than just having a will. Preparation of the next generation (known as 'heir conditioning') is important, as is providing estate liquidity to cover probate costs, organising documents and copies of the will and thinking through the tax implications of your estate. A will is an absolutely necessary part of estate preparation but is not, in itself, sufficient.

ACHIEVING YOUR OBJECTIVES

The most important part of a Wealth Wisdom Plan is the achievement of results. The questions and answers above can only provide guidance to you for your own personal financial journey.

A Wealth Wisdom Plan can help you to define your overall vision, to clarify the objectives and targets you set for yourself and can help to set out an approach to give you control over all elements of your financial life.

The responsibility, the credit and the benefits of designing and implementing your financial plan are entirely yours.

With a clear and intelligent plan, coupled with the discipline to stick to that plan, you will be able to achieve far more than you might by a less thoughtful, less disciplined and more random approach to wealth management.

If you feel you did not do a perfect job the first time through, do not be worried. The important thing is that by setting out on the journey toward excellence in financial management, you will have taken a giant step toward the goal of ensuring that you are fully in control of your own financial future.

We wish you well in your endeavours.

I. ANNUAL BUDGET	A. Monthly Payment	B. Full Year = Monthly × 12	C. Non-Monthly Payments	D. Total (= B + C)
Income				
Salary and Bonus				
Other Income				
(minus Public Pension Deductions)				
(minus Income Tax)				
Net Income				
Expenses				
Housing				
Utilities				
Transportation				
Telephone and Internet				
Fees and Interest on Credit Cards and Loans				
Insurance				
Medical Care				
Groceries and Restaurants				
Education				
Personal Expenses				
Vacations				
Charity				
Gifts				
Domestic Help				
Contingency				
Other				
Total Expenses				
Available for Savings and Investment (= Net Income minus Total Expenses)				

III. PERSONAL WEALTH SCHEDULE

Personal Investment Profile (circle one for each category)

Time Frame	short	medium	long
Risk Appetite	low	medium	high
Liquidity Preference	high	medium	low
Savings Rate	low	medium	high
Contingency Needs	high	medium	low

Wealth Objectives

1.

2.

3.

Savings & Investment Portfolio	Last year	This year	Next year
Property Value			
(minus Mortgage)			
Net Property Value (Property Value minus Mortgage)			

	Last year	This year	Next year
Cash and Deposits			
Own Business			
Shares			
Bonds			
Mutual Funds			
Public Pension			
Private Pension			
Foreign Currency Accounts			
Gold and Commodities			
Arts and Antiques			
Private Equity			
Derivatives and Hedge Funds			
Insurance Investments			

Chart ❦ 263

Educational Funds			
Other			
Total Savingsand Investment			

Total Non-Mortgage Debts			

Personal Wealth (= Net Property Value plus Total Savings and Investments minus Total Non-Mortgage Debts)			

II. MONTHLY BUDGET TRACKER	Monthly Budget	Jan	Feb	Mar	Apr	May	Jun	Jul	Aug	Sep	Oct	Nov	Dec	Total This Year
Income														
Salary and Bonus														
Other Income														
(minus Public Pension Deductions)														
(minus Income Tax)														
Net Income														
Expenses														
Housing														
Utilities														
Transportation														
Telephone and Internet														
Fees and Interest on Credit Cards and Loans														
Insurance														
Medical Care														
Groceries and Restaurants														
Education														
Personal Expenses														
Vacations														
Charity														
Gifts														
Domestic Help														
Contingency														
Other														
Total Expenses														

Available for Savings and Investment
(= Net Income minus Total Expenses)

Printed in the United States
by Baker & Taylor Publisher Services